Digital Cultures

Digital
Cultures

MILAD DOUEIHI

Harvard University Press

Cambridge, Massachusetts, and London, England

2011

First published as *La grande conversion numérique*, copyright © Editions du Seuil, 2008 and 2009. Collection *La Librairie du XXIe siècle* dirigée par Maurice Olender.

Library of Congress Cataloging-in-Publication Data
Doueihi, Milad.
  [Grande conversion numérique. English]
  Digital cultures / Milad Doueihi. — American ed.
    p. cm.
  Includes bibliographical references and index.
  ISBN 978-0-674-05524-7 (alk. paper)
    1. Information society.   2. Digital divide.   3. Digital media—Social aspects.
  4. Information technology—Social aspects.   I. Title.
  HM851.D677813 2011
  303.48'33—dc22   2010032972

Our inheritance proceeds from no testament.

René Char, *Feuillets d'Hypnos*

Contents

Note to the American Edition

This book, written in late 2006, appeared first in a French translation published by Le Seuil in early 2008. While the temptation is great, especially with the rapid evolution of digital culture and the emergence of Web 2.0 and associated tools and practices, I have chosen not to modify the original, except for some minor corrections. For the main objective of the book is to articulate, through the diversity of digital practices, the need for a rich understanding of digital literacy and the emergence of a literate environment that is essentially founded on an anthological practice. If anything, the current trends seem to confirm such an interpretation.

Digital literacy embodies the radical changes brought about by the socioeconomic impact of the new technology. While it is useful to think of it through an analogy with the literacy associated with print and the culture of the book, it is equally important to take into account the full power of their differences. With the digital, it is not sufficient, at least in my opinion, to reduce literacy to a minimalist familiarity with the tools and their exploitation. Instead, we need to rethink some of our received models, so embedded within print and its powerful heritage (both cultural and legal), in order to better appreciate the new dimensions of digital culture. In the same manner that digital tools disturb our received ideas about authorship and reading, digital literacy invites a new look and an evaluation of what it means to be literate. In the digital environment, more so than at any other moment in the past, literacy is the agency not only of communication and the production and exchange of knowledge; it is also the site of the deployment of a new iteration of individual and collective identities. In this fashion, it is also the site of a conflict, one opposing our inherited practices and their powerful history and the emerging new world of digital culture.

In this context, I chose to focus on some of the similarities between scholarly, learned, and literary traditions and some of the most visible characteristics of digital practices. Thus, in the first place, we see the importance of the anthological, but also of forms of religious belief and the ways in which they structure group identity and encourage the production of diversity.

Why an anthological practice? Simply because it would seem that the fragment, the basic element of an anthology, is the most appropriate form and format of the digital age. An anthology is constituted by assembling various pieces of material under a unifying cover, and for the use of an individual or a group brought together by a common interest. The new sociability associated with today's social networks is mostly populated by anthologies circulating between groups of friends and contacts, and ones that are often themselves formed by references to other existing anthologies.[1] One key feature of the anthological is the dissociation between text, on the one hand, and authorship and intentionality, on the other. It makes it possible for a free and unforeseen circulation of information in new contexts, thus allowing for either a form of dull repetition, one that can resemble rumor, or, more interestingly, the creation of new and surprising forms of knowledge. One thing is certain, however: the anthological, because of its fragmentary nature, raises important questions about our forms of access and interface with historical archives, whether textual or otherwise.[2] At the same time, it points to the fragility of the editorial models inherited from print culture. While it has become commonplace to repeat that the digital collapses or at least minimizes the difference between author and reader, the anthological highlights a renaissance of the empowered reader: a reader already an author, but an author within the limits and constraints imposed by the tools; thus the centrality of digital literacy.

A second dimension of the new digital culture hinted at but not fully developed in the book relates to the relations between digital technology and the body.[3] We are currently witnessing the emergence of a virtual urbanism, a hybrid urbanism that is literally reshaping our environment. Urbanists know all too well that man is defined by language as well as by his relation to space, and the so-called virtual worlds, whether they be games, social networks, or augmented reality, offer a new opportunity for human architecture. This virtual urbanism began with a return of the voice associated with the success of podcasting and digital radio and has since been reinforced by the convergence of cloud computing and the mobile networks, since the arrival of tactile screens. But also, we can say that digital culture began as a culture of the office and the chair and has since become a culture of mobility: we read and write while walking or in our vehicles. Such a change is highly significant, for we know, at least since Marcel Mauss, that the nature of cultural objects is closely related to the position of the body in a culture. Thus we are on the verge of a new, hybrid cultural landscape.[4] *Digital Cultures* is one of many ways of approaching and understanding our present.

Preface

Let me begin with a confession: I am neither a computer scientist nor a technologist. Nor am I a lawyer who specializes in intellectual property and the intricacies of copyright. I consider myself an accidental digitician, simply a computer user who has followed the changes in the digital environment over the last twenty years. By profession I am what you would call a philologist and an intellectual historian, someone who normally spends his time thinking about words and concepts, their meanings, and the ways they shape some of our perceptions and inform our ideas about ourselves and the world around us. I am interested in all dimensions of literacy and the ways in which it makes possible the formulation of information, and its subsequent transformation into knowledge as much as in the manner in which it produces the categories and concepts for ordering, organizing, and transmitting our knowledge. From my point of view, digital culture represents a unique instance for the intellectual historian to interact with and observe momentous changes that have produced large-scale practices that are rapidly putting into place new cultural norms that challenge well-established conventions and traditions deeply embedded in the literacy and economy of print culture and its sociopolitical framework.

As an accidental digitician, I have often experienced a sense of frustration and misrecognition: a frustration because frequently enough, the discourse on digital matters is dominated by technologists and lawyers to the exclusion of a humanistic voice (humanistic in the sense of a discourse of the Humanities).[1] Many of the current American and European debates concerning the impact of digital culture on the legal framework have been conducted by technologists and lawyers, all vying for the attention of legislators in order to influence the formulation of the legal texts that are meant to govern the rapidly changing cultural and social practices made possible by the digital environment. While such a state of affairs is neither surprising nor necessarily undesirable, it is striking to observe the absence of an active humanistic participation in this crucial debate. For reasons that remain to be investigated, the Humanities as a discipline have been sidelined into a marginal position in a debate whose central terms and defining concepts derive in large part from humanistic practices with their complex and often ignored, if not forgotten, histories.[2] It would seem as if digital culture, in the current political and cultural environment, is detached from its own not so distant history by the apparent need for a speedy legal fix for the problems it raises. And yet an essential part of the vocabulary of the debate stirring the current "culture wars" is a debate focused on ideas about the legitimacy of practices and norms that are themselves grounded in a literary and literate culture. To simplify, one can say that the digital environment is at the moment experiencing a crisis derived from its early reliance and desire to carry over and extend elements of print culture (such as embedded and legal forms of authorship, copyright, but also crucial concepts such as page, book, and the notions of property associated with them) into its own, and from its current desire, in part due to the development of new technologies and their associated emerging practices, to liberate itself from the weight of such a burden. The absence of a historical voice in this debate is most striking, and despite some admirable legal and technological discourses, there is room, I believe, for a contribution that does not shy away from the historical and even the philological, while being informed and comfortable within the digital environment itself. In other words, the book that follows is meant as a reflection on the conditions for the emergence of a *new literacy*—a digital literacy—that is not simply a numeracy, nor is it a set of norms for manipulating a technology.[3] This digital literacy is not only defining new socioeconomic realities but is also articulating critical if not radical modifications of a set of abstractions and concepts operative in our broad social, cultural, and political horizons—identity, location, territory and jurisdiction, presence and location, community and individuality, ownership, archives, and so on.

Digital literacy transmits a social imaginary that puts into play not only the virtual dimension of the new technologies but also religious, historical, and political assumptions and prejudices that shape the new culture as much and perhaps with even more power and influence than the mere access to the same technology across national and cultural borders. In a sense, as we shall see later, the digital environment, while acting as a new, and for some, universal, civilizing process (the sometimes facile global dimension of digital technology), is also inhabited by specific practices and well-defined forms of knowledge that require closer inspection and call for a comparative examination of past models. It is marked by historically dense ideas about the management of knowledge and its transmission, by the weight given to rationality and by the specificities of voice and presence and their manifestation within the technological boundaries of the environment.

Numeracy, it can be argued, is unmotivated (although that remains an open question). If indeed numeracy is blind in its intent and impact, the digital is, on the other hand, first and foremost cultural and historical. And the eminence of legal and technological discourses in the current debates about the future management of the digital environment points to an absence that can only be filled by a broadly defined cultural voice. This book aims at providing one such voice.

The second dimension of the experience of the accidental digitician is misrecognition of identity. I recall former colleagues' remarks when passing by my office, intrigued and disturbed by my prominently omnipresent computer: When are you going to stop playing and do some real work? As if digital culture were simply an add-on, a curiosity and a distraction, a superfluous item having no relation to the "real work" a scholar is supposed to be doing. This book is a belated answer to this reproach in that it seeks to demonstrate the need and hopefully the relevance of a reflection on digital culture and its environment informed by the literary and the historical.

The divide between traditional historical intellectual disciplines and the cultural realities of advanced technological and knowledge-based societies does not imply the possible loss or disappearance of the human factor or identity in the new digital reality. Instead, it invites us to reflect on the dynamic relations between culture and technology, and to think through current technological innovations and the social practices they make possible with the tools of cultural history. It is thus a dialogue between the "old" and the current, between the historical and the emerging present, and ultimately a reflection on whether digital technology is to be thought of in universal if not universalist terms, outside the boundaries and baggage of specific historical and social contexts. We need to ask whether the spread of digital culture implies the collapse of local specificities and identities, or whether the universalist claim is instead driven by the need of (national) jurisdictions to assert their authority and the legitimacy of their economic and political vocabulary, thus reinforcing their legal control over intellectual property rights and over the exchange and transmission of new forms of information. Such a drive manifests an increased desire on the part of the legal authorities to track and manage digital identity. Today the tension between such universalist drives characterizes the struggle for the new political discourse that is meant to set the broad terms for the management of the new digital environment. This tension, I will argue, reveals the fragility of both the key concepts at stake as well as the legal framework developed to manage them. Once challenged by practices that are out of the immediate control of the legislative process, the legal machine (and the technological machine as well) is forced to try to enforce new controls, supposed to uphold the credibility and the acceptability of emerging practices. But such efforts, as we have seen over the last few years, are doomed to failure because they ignore what I call the cultural bias essential to these new practices, that is to say, their power to generate both coherent justifications and, especially, legitimate accounts of why they challenge the established rules and norms, disturbing the tranquility of the legal protections of intellectual property with all its economic and social implications. For one of the most promising, yet to some, troubling aspects of the digital environment lies in its immediate impact on the wider culture and its rapid and almost irresistible reshaping of cultural values. The digital environment is first and foremost a culture of rapid change and adaptability: it is a cultural phenomenon driven by social adaptations of technological innovations, and thus it calls for a dual inquiry into its inner mechanisms and structures. This dual perspective will need to be both descriptive and analytic, both technical and cultural.

Because of its humanistic perspective, this cultural discussion may appear naïve if not irrelevant to some lawyers and technologists. And because of its respect for the importance of the technological itself, it also runs the risk of alienating historians and some social scientists. However, this risk is worth taking because the overwhelming majority of users are simply that: users and not experts in one field or another; and yet, as such, they define what becomes the norm while they are subjected to the often uninformed opinions and decisions of experts unwilling to venture outside of the limits of their areas of specialization. In business, it is accepted wisdom to say that the customer is always right. But this is not the case in the digital environment. The user is not only not always right; he or she is subject to increasingly draconian control. And yet this is the environment whose culture is by definition flexible and modifiable. But increasingly, only informed users are able to challenge and modify the prefabricated digital environment they are offered. This trend is perhaps best illustrated by the growing importance of "Web" environments where modifications and personalization are relatively manageable and more easily controlled by providers (not to mention the thorny question of content ownership). But nevertheless, between the online and desktop environments and their richer linkage, the tools for such a change are drawn from the larger cultural environment. And the individual capable of carrying out such a modification is what I call a literate digitician.

But where do we get the literate digiticians? At this point in time they are nearly all a product of accident. Most accidental digiticians recognize themselves easily: they are the new "experts," the local and accidental experts. They are the ones who find themselves in charge of fixing and maintaining a number of computers for family members and friends. Always on call when a problem occurs, they tend to spend good parts of dinner parties in the study inspecting a dear friend's latest blunder, configuring a protected wireless network for a neighbor, upgrading a machine or eliminating spyware from a brother-in-law's crippled desktop. In short, they are the unacknowledged members of a self-organizing civil rescue team that tries to protect against cyber thieves and their endless stream of increasingly sophisticated attacks. The accidental digiticians bridge the gap between users and programmers, between technologists and lawyers, between specialists and consumers. They hail from all walks of life: librarians, retired military officers, artists, unemployed, and so forth. They are informed about the latest technologies without being creators of technologies. But the accidental digitician is also the soldier, or better yet the preacher of literacy, of the new digital literacy, spreading the word, as it were, to their local communities. They are responsible for "converting" friends and acquaintances to systems or platforms they advocate, to new tools and new practices, to new realities and new forms of presence that shape distributed communities. Their reward is often a kind word or a vintage bottle of wine from a grateful soul lost in the maze of digital options.

The accidental digiticians embody the position outlined by Michel de Certeau in his *La culture au pluriel*, an unauthorized position from which one can freely discuss digital culture, without the necessary constraints of the experts' language or the restrictions of the specialists' discourse: "Nothing authorizes me to speak of culture; I have no credentials. So, my own intellectual positions by their very nature make room for different beliefs and different analyses. It therefore becomes possible to address frankly some of the dangerous questions that the so-called qualified experts try to avoid. An attitude of refined reticence would lead straight into academicism."[4] They speak *with* prejudice and do not shy away from it, allowing thus for an open and active debate about digital culture. They are the unacknowledged minority who to a large degree keep the digital environment functional and accessible.

The text that follows is an *essay* on digital culture and its literacy. It certainly does not aim to be an exhaustive presentation of current technologies or an all-inclusive survey of digital practices.

Since most of the material discussed is available online, and because of the nature of online references and their at times unfortunate impermanence, all citations were verified as of September 17, 2007.

Digital Cultures

Introduction:
A New Civilizing
Process?

Civility has always been an issue and a concern in the online world. From the early days of Usenet and its various successors (Bulletin Boards, Mailing Lists, etc.) to the current, rich Web environments that include group authoring and sharing tools to Chat systems and, more recently, VOIP calling and messaging, an initially implicit set of conventions has slowly emerged into a set of detailed guides for good online citizenship. The first of these, known as Netiquette captures, is, in its title alone, the convergence of a networked environment with the need for a minimal set of rules for the good functioning of a distributed forum that has made it possible for Web culture to develop in the manner of a civilizing process. While the evolution of Netiquette mirrors the changes in the nature of the digital environment itself, my purpose in these introductory remarks is not to provide a history of online civility nor to follow its mutations in order to capture the shifting sociology of the digital environment. Instead, I would like to reflect on some of the implications of civility for the digital environments, implications that run much deeper than simply maintaining a viable and functional online space. For civility, as Norbert Elias has shown, is constituted by a set of practices and managed expectations that shape the manifestation of individual presence and its place within a controlled hierarchy.[1] The civilizing process is not only the emergence of social norms that have the power to link meaning to established hierarchies (and here the current digital environment is filled with examples of such normalizing effects); it is also the agent of "affect" management and, more importantly for our purposes, of new rules for both self-management and for the control and surveillance of individualistic expressions, especially dissenting ones. It is in this context that we grasp the broader significance of online civility and of the digital environment as *habitus* and its relations to some of the major concerns raised by the phenomenal growth of digital culture, namely, privacy and security.

In this respect, the digital environment, in its global drive, while allowing for increased access and, in some cases, for much needed freedoms, introduces new and powerful modes of surveillance and censorship. In other words, digital culture functions much like a civilizing process, bringing along with it new opportunities as well as unpredictable and at times disturbing if not dangerous side effects. Such a situation is in large part a reflection of the social nature of the digital environment and of the associated need for managing and regulating it. But the reader may wonder why I refer to digital culture as a civilizing process and what the consequences of such a choice are. While it is true, as illustrated by Netiquette, that this culture has always had its manners and protocols mostly born out of a combination of practical and historical conventions as much as the opportunities provided by the technology itself and its evolution, the norms for acceptance and membership in online groups contain the elements of digital identity and the group dynamics it make possible. In other words, under the guise of civility, we have the defining principles (always mutating due to the changes in technology as much as the growth and diversity of the membership) for a new and initially parallel social order detached from national origin, or what we might call conventional identity. This virtual social order, in recent times, lays claim to a universality grounded in the perceived "neutral" nature of the technology and its reception. But this universality, for its coherence and intelligibility, relies on the notion of digital identity. In other words, digital culture, due in part to its success and its ever important economic role, operates a shift and a transition that are both political and sociological and ultimately cultural. It is in this respect that we can compare the rise of digital culture and its universalist tendency to religion. In fact, I would argue that currently, digital culture is the *only* rival to religion as a universal presence.

The much discussed and celebrated transition from analog to digital and all that it entails amounts to a *conversion*, in the technical as much as the religious sense of the term. And conversion requires a retrospective examination of the past (thus the reinterpretation and recapturing of older frameworks and contents into the new ones) as well as new explanations of actions and events. It is precisely because of this seemingly inevitable process of conversion that digital culture, no matter how vaguely we define it, is laying a claim for the status of an equivalent of a world religion with its prophets and priesthood, its institutions and sects and believers, its dissenters and schismatics.[2] It has its own language that has infiltrated and begun to reshape the spoken and written languages (think, for an example, of the influence of SMS on our linguistic practices and of the online-inspired typography, the use of capitals, etc.).[3] Our learned literacy is slowly but surely under the influence of the emerging practices of digital literacy. A civilizing process that is also a religious phenomenon is indeed a powerful agent of cultural change. But it can also become a dangerous agent that blinds its subjects to its limitations and ultimately to what it makes inaccessible if not irrelevant and unintelligible.

Already in the late fifties, Jacques Ellul, in his pioneering work on the culture of technology, pointed out some of these discursive dangers: "Indeed, no one is capable of making a true and itemized account of the total effect of existing techniques."[4] Indeed, for Ellul, *Technique* (and for us the digital environment is the most powerful embodiment of what Ellul calls *Technique*) is characterized by a number of features that distinguish it from all other cultural phenomena. It is ultimately marked by a dehumanizing, and as we shall see, antireligious tendency that results from the automation of technical choices (in other words, the choices offered to users and agents are a function of technological evolution independent of the needs or desires of users), and the associated self-produced evolution.[5] From Ellul's analysis, it emerges that the inherent nature of technology, and especially of digital technology, while expanding for its own internal reasons and purposes, promises an ever-improving environment and greater free-doms, albeit ones that are subject to the need to address the growing num-ber of complex technological problems and difficulties. Thus, internal technological constraints shape and often restrict human practices. Fur-thermore, the universalist dimension of digital culture leads to a valoriza-tion of uniformity, to a code under which similarity becomes the rule. A new civility thus emerges, one that engineers the management of pres-ence and of the digital representation of the individual in terms of the technological reality, if not realism.

While this assessment may seem overly pessimistic, I think it is fair to point out that despite some deployments of digital technology that take into account local specificities and cultural identities, the overall impact of the digital "gold rush" is most distinguished by an impoverishment of diversity for the sake either of conformity or, more frequently, of economic competitiveness. The religious dimension of digital culture produces a flattening of differences and the reduction of local factors and variables to mere superficial variations on the universal and homogeneous technologi-cal culture and its digital environment. In short, the digital promised land is a digital utopia that will always be undermined by its technological overdetermination. Digital culture, owing in part to its surreptitious hold on the new and universal civility it propagates, transforms itself from the agency of specific cultural and political identities into the agency of iden-tity. It translates its necessary and seemingly irresistible penetration into all public and private spheres into the technique for reshaping and defin-ing a new civilization. For Ellul, this technological drive constitutes the main and most dangerous feature of Technique:

> Herein lies the inversion we are witnessing. Without exception in the course of history, technique belonged to a civilization and was merely a single element among a host of nontechnical activities. Today tech-nique has taken over the whole of civilization. Certainly technique is no longer the simple machine substitute for human labor. It has come to be the "intervention into the very substance not only of the in-organic but also of the organic."[6]

Digital culture and its ever-changing environment thus need to be ex-amined as a set of discursive practices, with their own conventions and norms that tend to fragilize and disturb well-established categories and values. Some of these categories or concepts are easily recognizable: a set of notions that are part of print culture and that were at the center of our negotiations with intellectual property (copyright, *droits d'auteur*, authorship, etc.); a geographical and genealogical representation of identity (tied to nationality, jurisdiction, etc.). Others are more complex and more subtle because they reflect local traditions and diverse legal and cultural developments. Thus, for instance, privacy, which, at least in the United States, is conventionally a spatial representation (the individual private sphere is a home marked by boundaries). It goes without saying that digital privacy problematizes such a conception, which explains the current difficulties in formulating acceptable and balanced rules for addressing the thorny issues raised by the need to protect it. New definitions of privacy, grounded in the transformations introduced by digital culture, are necessary in order to address the need for a balanced approach to privacy abuses. Furthermore (and we shall return to this question later), privacy, in the digital environment, is intimately tied to security, and thus requires an examination of its social dimensions as well as of its economic cost. Owing to the nature of digital culture, privacy, much like security, is a question of risk and trust. Digital privacy puts into place a complex network of personalization of presence and of trusted entities that have access and are supposed to shield and protect sensitive and private information. And yet such a trusted entity, and again owing to the nature of the digital environment itself (networked and distributed and therefore vulnerable to infiltration), is subject to increased security risk and breaches, as witnessed by the growing unauthorized access to private information hosted by either government agencies or private institutions. While such breaches are ultimately unavoidable (but they can be reduced in numbers), they point out the inherent difficulties faced by the digital environment when it comes to providing a relatively stable context for identity.[7]

If digital culture is slowly but surely modifying some of the essential conceptual tools of our current world, it is also facing a growing number of difficult problems in its quest for normalization. On the one hand, it is reshaping jurisdictions (for example, the jurisdictional breakdown brought about by the distributed nature of the network and the inability of conventional laws to reach their digital subjects beyond their national borders) to such a degree that it ultimately invites their reinforcement, and, on the other, it relies on a uniform discursivity that only now is beginning to face some significant opposition and challenges. The tentatively emerging regional, ethnic, or linguistically specific digital environments are meant to resist the jurisdictional reshaping driven by the desire to control the digital economics of intellectual property. It is not surprising, considering the financial stakes, that copyright laws have become, at least for the United States, a tool for diplomatic and commercial negotiations. For the need of a globally coherent and cohesive legal framework for the new forms of ownership faces an opposition grounded in the practices made possible by the technology itself. If the technology makes it easily possible to copy, convert, and transfer any digital object, the law tries to control and regulate such a freedom. It does so in part by its efforts to manage digital identity, even in its current rudimentary form.

But digital identity is fundamentally polyphonic[8] and as such it makes possible a multiplicity and a diversity that, while attracting efforts to standardize and profile them, will always challenge and resist an absolutist form of control. In other words, the polyphonic dimension of digital identity has the *potential* to embed diverse cultural specificities within digital culture and thus possibly relativize and minimize its universalist tendency. If digital culture is a new religion, digital identity can best resist its influence. At the same time, the polyphony of digital identity plays an important role in a nexus of crucial categories: the interaction between the digital and the political (from electronic voting and its required minimal digital literacy as well as the security concerns it raises, to the ways in which politics has been influenced and at times reshaped by the digital environment) and the forms of political actions that will emerge from such an interaction; emergent forms of responsibility that will have to forge their path between the social and its needs and the digital and its potential and limitations; emergent forms of economic frameworks and business models better-adapted to the nature of the digital object and consistent with digital practices and usages; and finally, to limit oneself to the broadest and most important elements, the new emergent values that will determine the transformation and information into knowledge in the future.

If digital culture is the carrier of new paradigms of knowledge and identity, it is also the site of a conflictual contest of paradigms of credibility and legitimacy.[9] Often enough, governments and authorities (except in countries with authoritarian regimes) are simply playing catch-up with the implications of adoption of ever-changing digital tools. But beyond this divide, the contest of credibility and legitimacy I mention here is more related to both the scope of digital culture, its values and valorizations and, finally and most importantly, the role of rationality in determining cultural orientation.[10] For underlying most evaluations of the impact and structure of the digital environment (by structure here I mean the organization and order of the network, its hubs and nodes and their relations, its overall geography as well as its modes of producing meaning) are models grounded in rational representations of human organizations.[11] Such models, in their attention to the weight of the group and the role played by the collective, tend to minimize the status of the individual and the exceptional. In a way, they illustrate what troubles most critics of technology from Heidegger to Ellul,[12] for they highlight either the disappearance of the human subject or the overwhelming influence of what Heidegger describes as the "activité violente du savoir" embodied by *Techné*.[13] Between a lucid anxiety in the face of the rise of the culture of Technique for Ellul and, on the other hand, the metaphysical concern expressed by Heidegger for the reduction of philosophy to a simple philosophy of nature, to an interrogation of *Phusis*, to a meditation on what is only an object instead of the language of Being, how do we assess the new digital epistemology and its displacement of the human? How are we to account for its unequalled success despite its very ambivalence (or the impossibility, within the digital, to easily and clearly distinguish between the true and the false)? How can we understand the new divide between digital perfectibility, anchored as it is in repetition and reproducibility and the accompanying mutation of values and norms and their ethical dimension?

The new civility inaugurated by digital culture has its new ecosystem with its internally defined notion of progress. Furthermore, at least in its current state, it would seem to privilege usage above all, thus opting for presence over analysis, for location over substance, for visibility over relevance. Such norms have their own metrics and, to paraphrase Ellul, their own algebra: they are driven by an economic imperative that is oriented toward the infinitely (or statistically) large. As such, digital culture has its own aesthetics (and here it suffices to recall that the Sublime was always divided between the infinite and the infinitesimally small). But I would like to conclude these introductory remarks by situating what, beyond the aesthetic feature of the networked environments, has been frequently called, in many quarters, the *posthuman* as a consequence of the digital age, for it represents the ultimate expression of the new civilization inaugurated by the digital. The posthuman is, normally, a reference to the convergence of machine and man, to the possibility of intersection, within the body, of mind and computer. It designates the hybrid that could, theoretically, emerge from the potential of nanotechnology and its deployment in the human body. Moreover, the posthuman stands as the perfect incarnation of the new individual generated by what I characterize as the religious dimension of digital culture. Furthermore, it is the culmination of a debate about the nature of intelligence, of human intelligence and of its recuperation if not augmentation by the digital machine. As such, it stands as the extreme form of a potential digital civilization that would signal the eclipse of the old order and the rise of a new age, frequently imagined and described in science fiction and now apparently approaching potential realization. It will not be surprising to find that behind the debates about machine and intelligence lies a dispute about culture, its role and status in the digital future, and its complex relations to automation.

For those who wonder why I insist on such a dimension of the digital, I will only point out that underlying the current debates on Artificial Intelligence and the posthuman are concerns that we are most familiar with, in society at large as well as in the learned communities. Any discussion of the nature and origin of intelligence, of its intimate association with the human as a source and a model; any examination of the key concepts of autonomy, of subjectivity, of individuality in their history and in relation to the dynamic interaction between a human and his environment, raises not only philosophical questions about identity and the nature of the human and its current evolution, but also ethical dilemmas that reflect social and economic concerns that are, in the final analysis, religious or derived from our religious heritage. Within this complex network, digital culture plays a determining role in normalizing forms of intelligence, but it also raises the risk of reducing intelligence to a more unified and homogeneous notion defined in large part by the digital context itself. In other words, digital culture can, by its universalist drive, privilege one form of intelligence over a diversity that currently exists.

The debate about re-creating intelligence or creating autonomous adaptive intelligence in the digital age recalls the one that was occasioned by the publication of Michel Foucault's *Les Mots et les Choses* in 1966.[14] The dreaded "death of man" and the "disappearance of the subject" generated much controversy and debate. But, to stay with Foucault's own work and evolution, it culminated, in this perspective, in his inaugural lecture at the Collège de France, *L'ordre du discours*, a text that is ultimately devoted to the notion of literary authorship and to the relations between acts of speech and their legal and institutional representations.[15] The meditation on the evolution and status of the subject is thus intimately tied to the problem of the figure of the author, of its history and relations to print culture, and its materialities as much as its imaginary or symbolic production. In the same manner, the research and conversations about intelligence are intimately linked to the human and its environment, to the understanding of intelligence as an interaction with a context, one with a history and a rich and strong heritage. In both cases language is central: for the humanistic and historical disciplines, discursive authorship in all its diversity lies at the core of the analysis of cultural productions, and, by the same token, for the engineer and the computer scientist (and, ultimately robot designer and creator), language learning and discursive adaptive skills provide the norm and the measure of success of the design and deployment of what Luc Steels has beautifully termed Digital Angels.[16] For him, the robots of the feature are much like mythological figures, but with different corporealities: "perhaps an appropriate metaphor for what the robots of the future will be like is related to the age-old mythological concept of angels. Almost every culture has imagined persistent beings which help humans through their life. These beings are ascribed cognitive powers, often beyond those of humans, and are supposed to be able to perceive and act in the real world by materializing themselves in a bodily form at will. . . . Of course, in mythologies there are not only angels but also devils. We just have to make sure that our world gets populated by angels!"[17] What Steels identifies as "mythological" I call "religious." And at the heart of the scientific and computational component of the digital we encounter the narrative function of the religious in its capacity to provide models for not only the origin but also the future of the human if not the posthuman.

Digital Angels are perhaps the expression of the emerging reality born of digital culture, but Steels's subtle view of artificial intelligence and its future is only one among many.[18] On the other side, we have the work of Ray Kurzweil, the author of *The Age of Spiritual Machines* and, in its updated version, *The Singularity Is Near.*[19] Kurzweil is the proponent and the prophet of the ultimate digital and technological age. For him, science and technology are on the verge of solving the mysteries of intelligence and of radically transforming human history. Unlike Steels, he is firmly optimistic about the nature of the future:

This merger of man and machine, coupled with the sudden explosion in machine intelligence and rapid innovation in the fields of gene research as well as nanotechnology, will result in a world where there is no distinction between the biological and the mechanical, or between physical and virtual reality. These technological revolutions will allow us to transcend our frail bodies with all their limitations. Illness, as we know it, will be eradicated. Through the use of nanotechnology, we will be able to manufacture almost any physical product upon demand, world hunger and poverty will be solved, and pollution will vanish. Human existence will undergo a quantum leap in evolution. We will be able to live as long as we choose. The coming into being of such a world is, in essence, the Singularity.[20]

Kurzweil's scenario reads like the latest utopia, in which science fiction becomes reality, but without either the stereotypical, out-of-control and violent robot that disturbs the idyllic life made possible by technology or the intrusive potential of the technology, especially when it merges with the human body.

Such a look at some of the future scenarios for digital technology is instructive because it invites us to consider further and with more care its current state, its historical density, and its potential for redefining the human environment. In this book, by focusing on some of today's more widespread technologies, I attempt to present a view of digital culture that explicitly privileges the *cultural*, in the broadest sense of the term, over the technical (while not, however, neglecting the technical). I undertake to discern, through the constraints as well as the opportunities opened up by the technology, the redeployment of rather classical models within the new environment. If we started with a simple evocation of etiquette and protocol, it is because such practices, as we know all too well, have the power to both order and subjugate, and also to invent new sites from which new knowledge can emerge. In other words, the digital environment that envelopes us promises to be a thrilling adventure for the one who can read and remember as well as interact with the machine and its evolving interfaces, but an adventure that, despite all of its newness, recalls and extends well-known models of intelligibility and sociability.

1

Digital Divides and the Emerging Digital Literacy

Perhaps a working definition of a key concept in this work is a good opening for a discussion of the nature and structure of the digital. What is digital culture, especially now that it has become so ubiquitous, so pervasive, and so familiar? Digital culture consists of a set of intertwined technologies that have produced and continue to produce social practices that, for the time being at least, either challenge or question the viability or even the legitimacy of some well-established social and cultural norms and their associated legal frameworks. Essentially, for our purposes in this chapter, I will say that digital culture is made up of communication and information exchange modes that displace, redefine, and reshape knowledge into new forms, formats, and the methods for acquiring and transmitting such knowledge. This rather abstract definition is useful, if only because it allows us to perceive directly something we experience implicitly all the time: digital culture requires new and ever-changing forms of literacy: digital literacy. Digital literacy goes well beyond the simple management of the available tools and the successful negotiation with the diversity of opportunities available for users today. It is, much like the literacy associated with print culture, rather dense and complex. And much like literacy, it has given rise to an initial reaction to its necessity or need and to what has been termed the "digital divide," echoing the differences between those who can read and those who cannot.

I. Between Print and Digital: A Conflict of Literacies?

Thus, it has become commonplace to discuss the so-called digital divide when we think about the impact of current technology on society.[1] The digital divide has been almost exclusively reduced to its socioeconomic manifestation and presumed causes, identifying it with the difference between those who have access to the various components of the digital environment and those who have not; between cultures and societies that are riding the wave of the new technologies and those that are either resisting it or left altogether outside of its scope of influence for either political or financial reasons. And yet we have neither a clear definition nor a coherent understanding of what we ultimately mean by this digital divide. At first look, the divide often mentioned by politicians and discussed in the popular press, especially in the United States and in Europe, is little more than an extension of a set of assumptions and inherited notions from the politics or the economics of an earlier era, whether it be the fight against poverty, illiteracy, or racism. This is simply to point out that we have tended, when trying to understand and address the issues raised by digital technology, to easily carry over conceptual structures that frame our understanding of emerging technologies and new paradigms of behavior. It is "natural" to do so because as a society we are fundamentally historical, and we learn from our previous experiences, adopting and adjusting our intellectual and legal horizons to adjust to new realities. It is also important to remember, however, that sometimes we continue to use some of these defining concepts too long or, especially, in a misplaced context; or that we resist modifying or abandoning some of them altogether simply because they have served us in the past, thus complicating and delaying our adaptation to the new realities put into place by new technologies or emergent cultural phenomena. This classical negotiation between the new and the old, between what has been tested and proven by experience and the fragility of the recent and the unknown, characterizes, in simple terms, how we change our collective practices in a relatively ordered manner, and how we have, so far, dealt with the challenges raised by the success of digital technology and its culture.

While the socioeconomic digital divide is important, sometimes its discussion is much too simplistic because it is dominated by immediate political concerns and justifications. As a counter example to its complete relevance, we can point out the rapid adoption and high rate of use of mobile phones and texting in economically underprivileged communities, and even more so in some underdeveloped nations. Therefore, we will find it useful to extend our definition of digital divide beyond this first stage in order to appreciate its intimate linkage with digital literacy and its implications for the future of digital culture.

Our first case will be the divide between the rapid technological growth and, more importantly, the associated cultural norms they produce and the legal framework meant to govern and regulate them. As an example here, we can point to the current state of copyright and intellectual property laws; the evolving nature of privacy and the need to adapt our privacy laws to make them better correspond to actual digital realities; and finally, linguistic and cultural digital identities and their corresponding "conventional" forms. On the copyright front, it would seem that legislative bodies (in the United States, in Europe, and in some Asian countries as well) are playing a futile catch-up game: they are formulating laws and policies that are based on either uninformed or outdated key concepts (and often entrenched interests) that are being radically redefined by the practical uses of today's technologies. In order to appreciate the significance of this legal divide, it is essential to point out that digital culture is an environment: it functions within a set of associated tools, modes of access, and the transferability between them. Digital environment means, in this context, the set of digital technologies and tools and the uses and practices they make possible along with the legal framework that is meant to manage them. Cultural digital practices, precisely because of the nature of their environment, pose some serious challenges to this all-too-familiar narrative of how laws try to catch up with technologies. And they do so in part because, for some (the majority of legislators, some publishers, etc.), they appear to be an extension of older and more familiar technologies and practices. Perhaps the most useful contrasts here are to be drawn from print culture or the culture of the book, because such examples illustrate best the usefulness as well as the problematic aspects of the intersections of the old and the new and the intertwining of the cultural and the technological, and because they touch upon the issues of copyright and intellectual property.

This conflation and extension (beyond its absolute continued relevance) of the fundamentals of print culture occur in part because, with the emergence of the first Web technologies, the dominant framing metaphor was reading. Thus we baptized the new tools as publishing instruments, producing Web pages, and relied on browsers to read those pages. Furthermore, the design and layout of the early Web tried to mimic the material qualities of the printed page (and some technologies continue to try to do so today). This is due in part to the robustness and flexibility of print, and to the power and cultural density of reading as a normative part of our culture. But the similarities between print and digital environments were also deceiving, not to say faulty. The Web, since its earliest days, and certainly today with the newer generation of "publishing" tools like blogs and especially Wiki, collapses the crucial distinction between author and reader in ways that are different from those possible within print culture, thus rendering the materiality of the page (as a possible indicator of its uniqueness or specificity) suspect at best and ultimately fragile if not irrelevant. The printed page is relatively fixed. It is associated with a work and an author. Its presentation is marked and is symbolically expressive (as, for instance, in the case of poetry: wide margins, spatial organization and presentation signify a genre in strictly formal terms). The digital "page" is both virtual and dynamic, and while it is often the work of an author, it is more easily assimilated by a reader who can modify it, reproduce it in another context, and transmit it in a variety of formats and versions. Furthermore, the printed page, in most cases, derives its meaning from a presupposed linear order, from the temporality of reading, whether continuous or fragmentary. The digital page, on the other hand, puts into place a different if not more complex and open-ended form of reading: it displays a virtuality that echoes that of the printed page, but it is only a virtuality, for the digital page is more spatial and access oriented. Furthermore, the digital page takes on different appearances or personalities, depending on how it is read, or, more precisely, in terms of what tools are used to read it. Even different browsers, or different versions of the same browser, can render the page differently, thus modifying its appearance and how it is or can be read. In short, the digital page "appears" to be a page, but in reality it is not, and this reality makes possible and actually calls for nonlinear forms of reading. The digital page, much like other digital entities, is a digital object that is characterized by its position within the digital environment and is not like either a manuscript or a printed page.

Perhaps a useful way to illustrate, concretely, this difference between the print and the digital is to consider RSS Aggregators as tools for accessing and reading online material (and this is even more important as all modern browsers have incorporated RSS support, thus extending the reader's freedom beyond the use of stand-alone Aggregators).[2] For our discussion in this chapter, I will retain only two features of Aggregators: the optional reader's control over the look and feel of the interface and the display of all recorded and archived edits of a page. Through simple, custom CSS (Cascading Style Sheets), the reader chooses his own look and feel and selects the overall layout and aesthetics of his interface with the material he is reading. Obviously, this is possible because the online page is a digital object, but it is also because of its position within the growing digital environments. As for the display of archived edits and modifications, some Aggregators allow readers to view the various levels of editorial interventions on a particular text, thus revealing, for the first time, the factors shaping the formulation of a particular news story.

The changes are color-coded, and an attentive reader can follow the history of every story, if it is available via RSS. While in this instance the story is not controversial, one can imagine the implications of such access to the archived version of the digital page of a politically sensitive story and where the editorial modifications can be interpreted as motivated. By the same token, the digital page forces the publisher, in this case a newspaper, to rethink both its editorial model and to reassess the design and presentation of its online paper, due to the pressures arising from the digital tools available to a significant number of users. In a sense, Aggregators enforce the difference between print and digital versions of the same text because they highlight the literacies they represent. There is, on the one hand, a relatively fixed model under which the author and producer is relatively in control of both content and format, and, on the other, a flexible format, based on the nature of the networked digital object, where the reader has the choice of becoming also author and editor or producer of information. In this case, the reader is more of a secret voyeur, a hidden observer of the inner workings of the publishing production, for he has gained access to what used to be privileged information. And along with this privilege comes new and different forms of readings.

But Aggregators are not restricted to desktop applications: they have become an integral part of most browsers and as such they also have begun to reshape the browsing experience. While it may be argued that Aggregators and RSS and Atom are essentially the glue that binds together the set of social computing tools (from blogs to Wikis and social-networking sites), it should be pointed out that, for the majority of users, Aggregators and the integration of RSS into browsers have the potential of increasing the autonomy of users and introducing an *alienation* into the online experience and presence.[3] Why alienation? Because autonomy, in this instance, encourages a passive form of reading or, more precisely, it can lead to a diminished form of interactivity between authors and readers, between sites and visitors. If a majority of readers choose to subscribe to sites' feeds, it is more than likely that they will find it harder to visit the sites, to comment, and to interact. It is true that you can subscribe to Comments' feeds, but if experience and studies are any indication, the tendency for most readers is simply to stay within the virtual environment provided by either Aggregators or browser RSS feeds In this fashion, we see again the significance of the distinction between two kinds of users, between users and manipulators, between the ones who will become, thanks to the new technologies, more passive and those who will become more vocal and ultimately play a stronger role in shaping not only technological evolution but also social and political agendas. The technology, as is often the case, contains the potential for significant change as well as for the introduction of new forms of isolation that is, curiously enough, based on the possibility of access to extensive information. Increased autonomy and the powers to control and manipulate the look and feel of information go hand in hand with a potentially significant form of withdrawal, of the institution of new forms of solitary experiences in the emerging virtuality of the network and its ever-larger expanse.

It goes without saying that Aggregators do not have to be used exclusively for accessing hidden archival edits or for passive readings of content. They can also be powerful research tools in the case of electronic "manuscripts" that can be thus studied genetically. And with the growing numbers of texts and books composed and published in formats accessible to Aggregators and similar tools, we are on the verge of a new era of authorship and readership.[4] But the rise and adoption of aggregation has also led, in some cases, to a somewhat utopian belief in the digital transformation of reading by digital technology. Such a belief is, however, based on the potential of technology to normalize cultural practices and activities and does not necessarily take into account the literate dimension of digital culture. Thus, for a prominent example, Bill Gates's recent comparison of the printed page and the computer screen:

> Reading is going to go completely online. We believe that as we get the smaller form factor, the screen has gotten good enough. Why is reading online better? It's up to date, you can navigate, you can follow links. The ads in the online reading are completely targeted as opposed to just being run-of-print, where many of the readers will find them completely irrelevant. The ads can be in new and richer formats. In fact the only drawbacks of the digital form are the things associated with the device: how big is it, how heavy is it, how many hours of power does it have, how much do I have to spend to buy it? But those are things that once you achieve that threshold, in terms of the convenience and the cost, then you see a dramatic change in behavior. Today, for people who read newspapers and magazines, even the most avid PC user probably still does quite a bit of reading on print. As the device moves down in size and simplicity, that will change, and so somewhere in the next five-year period we'll hit that transition point, and things will be even more dramatic than they are today.[5]

In this scenario, reading online is "better" because it simply deals with fresher and more up-to-date material. Reading, in this instance, is part and parcel of a "commercial" activity shaped by the nature of targeted advertisement and of the hyperlink structure of the network. What is lost, however, is the cultural density of the act of reading; what is forgotten in a somewhat blind faith in the linear powers of the technology is the potential for the emergence of specific literate forms of digital activity. The conclusions of a study of online reading habits and trends by the Poynter Institute reveals some fascinating results as to the current state of online reading.[6] The most surprising result was the fact that "a larger percentage of story text was read, on average, online than in print." And, again according to the study, online readers read about the same volume as their print counterparts. In other words, while digital culture presents a different format for readers, the practices of reading are not necessarily totally shaped by the technology. Instead, we are witnessing the emergence of a hybrid literacy, one that brings together the history of print culture and its reading activity and the new digital tools and their potential for transforming literacy altogether. In this context, aggregation is but a first symptom of such a transition into the new digital site for the new literacy. And if Aggregators are primarily reading tools, Wikis, which share some of their characteristics, carry this model into authoring itself.

II. Digital Rights or Digital Rights Management?

The weakening of the distinction between author and reader has wide-ranging implications that remain to be examined, and goes beyond a seemingly simple modification of the practice of reading. As we shall see later on in more detail, this fragilization is also an integral part of the emerging digital identity. Its importance is already being felt in our legal framework because it destabilizes copyright law (another inherited print culture concept), and will play an important role in reshaping universities and research institutions, or at least their management.

Universities and cultural institutions (museums, for instance) face a special if not unique set of copyright and IP- related problems, in part because of their history and in part owing to the nature of their mission and the expectations associated with their work, publications, and financial support (at least in the United States, but not exclusively so). Furthermore, it is clear that these institutions have responded in various degrees to the changes brought about by technological evolution and by the increased "visibility" of some of their production. The problem of intellectual property (IP) brings forth a conflict between the administration and the faculty and student body because it introduces, perhaps for the first time at such a significant scale, a divided interest between the traditional university constituencies. Learned communities with disciplinary rules and customs are now being challenged because of emerging technologies and the ways in which they destabilize some of the basic tenets of the older rules and procedures. Such procedures include the role of publications, especially online and Open Access publications, in recruiting and promoting faculty and researchers, the adjustments needed to take into account the realities of digital publishing and especially authorship. For museums (and we shall return to this question later in Chapter 4), the main difficulties arise from managing the digital versions of their holdings and negotiating an acceptable and pragmatic solution to the problem of copyright and intellectual property. If research universities are increasingly concerned with technology transfer, museums and similar cultural institutions need to address the thorny problem of conversion to the digital while respecting their public mission. In one instance, credibility and paradigms of legitimacy are at stake (for example, what is the status of refereed publishing in the age of Open Access?), whereas in the other, paradigms of sharing and making information and cultural products accessible are the key. In both cases, copyright and intellectual property are at the center of the debate and the changes undergone by the research and scholarly community as well as the cultural institutions in the digital age.

For copyright and intellectual property, it is, I believe, evident that a continuing defense and blind maintenance of the old system is ultimately futile, because it creates a cultural and economic discrepancy between what is ostensibly legal and what is accessible and possible, between what is legitimate and what is in use. It also has the potential of introducing differences between cultures and nations based on their respective copyright and intellectual property laws that will, at least in an initial phase, make it impossible to communicate freely between countries or to exchange material freely across the network. In other words, and we have already some efforts that threaten to put into place such conditions (in

France, for example), the divide we are discussing here, although it may appear at first simple and reduced to the potential of some digital tools, is capable of influencing national policies and laws. For this reason it is important to insist on the fact that the discrepancy between the print and digital environments, even in this overly simplified form, is one of the most important manifestations of the digital divide, because it designates the growing distance separating the more conventional ways of producing and sharing knowledge from the emerging paradigms of networked societies and the practices underlying them. The change in the nature of reading, initially embodied by digital tools, has obvious important economic consequences; as reading changes, so do the professions tied to it, from writing, editing, and publishing, to book selling. While we are currently in a transitional period that presents such professions with serious difficulties, it is not clear, at least for the foreseeable future, that the traditional book is really in danger. Reading online is not the same as reading a book: the two operations tend to be radically different. Online versions allow for speedy access to selected passages; reading tends to be segmented and fragmentary and tied to the need to cite; it is predominantly decontextualized and comparative (what I call "anthological," a feature we will discuss further later in this chapter). Most online readers prefer to own both print and digital versions of their books and this dualism is telling. The problems arise when the digital copies are locked, not allowing for relatively free access, and in this case, the majority of publishers have resisted even experimenting with open online formats for their digital books. Such resistance exemplifies the digital divide under discussion here, for it illustrates the refusal to acknowledge the reality and especially the extent to which the new digital culture has redefined the book and its traditions and institutions.

In a sense, we can think of this blockage and the continuing efforts in some quarters to introduce more stringent DRM (Digital Rights Management) on almost all digital objects, from books to movies and music, as a misunderstanding if not an economically motivated rejection of digital literacy. For in effect, DRM in all its forms, especially when it tries to shape the experience of the individual with the digital object and constrain the digital environment for allegedly economic reasons, amounts to the translation and the imposition of an insufficient and outdated model of literacy and its institutional and economic baggage on the emerging digital culture.

At its simplest, DRM identifies (via ISBN and similar standards that identify books, serials, music, recordings, film, etc.) intellectual property and provides a framework (a set of rules describing acceptable use) for the enforcement of usage restrictions or the exploitation of protected material. Such a framework requires international cooperation (in order to resolve jurisdictional issues) and an open set of standards that will ensure that systems and methodologies employed in developing component technologies remain interoperable. Furthermore, it necessitates the management of large-scale "control centers" in order to operate databases archiving relevant data covering purchased materials, users' rights and privileges, and distributors' management of protected material. As such, there is need for the standardization of the technical systems of identification of works and protected digital material (for instance, the Content Scrambling Scheme [CSS] was developed in Hollywood without any consultation with any other country or movie producers. Why should India and China, for instance, accept a privately developed technological scheme as the de facto standard for protecting and distributing digital films on DVDs? Also, why should other countries accept the regional scheme employed by CSS [CSS divides the world into seven regions, and DVDs are not compatible among regions]?).

It is important to recall that print has a simple yet overall very robust "Digital Rights Management" that relies on the nature of its object (the printed page and, especially the book as a vehicle that can incorporate effective protection measures). Initially, it was rather difficult and expensive to reproduce a print object in its entirety, and this technical obstacle served (with the exception of pirated editions, i.e., editions that were printed without the author's or the original editor's knowledge or consent). With the photocopier that changed, but it was still difficult to reproduce a book as such with ease. In brief, the robustness of the print model derives to a large measure from the nature of its format and its materiality, whereas the digital environment presents us with a diversity of formats that can, to the naked eye and ear, appear to be the same, and yet they are different objects. An MP3 file may sound like an AAC or WAV file, but they are distinct. It is the ease of conversion that complexifies rights and responsibilities in the digital age. It also shapes not only the regulation of legal distribution and exchange of material but also searching (a topic we will examine in some detail later on): How are libraries to store digital material? In their original format? Compressed? Or converted to some more efficient format (and here we encounter the problem of "conversion" raised briefly in the Introduction)? And if so, what is the status of the copyright protection that covers the original file and how does it extend to the converted files?

Just recently, Steve Jobs, Apple's CEO, argued for a music market that is effectively DRM free:

> The third alternative is to abolish DRMs entirely. Imagine a world where every online store sells DRM-free music encoded in open licensable formats. In such a world, any player can play music purchased from any store, and any store can sell music which is playable on all players. This is clearly the best alternative for consumers, and Apple would embrace it in a heartbeat. If the big four music companies would license Apple their music without the requirement that it be protected with a DRM, we would switch to selling only DRM-free music on our iTunes store. Every iPod ever made will play this DRM-free music.
>
> Why would the big four music companies agree to let Apple and others distribute their music without using DRM systems to protect it? The simplest answer is because DRMs haven't worked, and may never work, to halt music piracy. Though the big four music companies require that all their music sold online be protected with DRMs, these same music companies continue to sell billions of CDs a year which contain completely unprotected music. That's right! No DRM system was ever developed for the CD, so all the music distributed on CDs can be easily uploaded to the Internet, then (illegally) downloaded and played on any computer or player.[7]

The argument against DRM and its negative impact on the digital environment could not be made clearer, especially since it comes from the makers of the most successful DRM, FairPlay.[8] Even in financial terms, DRM is not a solution, as it is nothing more than a futile resistance to the

evolution of the culture and the constant breakdown of lock-down technologies.[9] Music DRM is perhaps the best illustration of the blindness
underlying the hesitation if not the refusal to see digital literacy as an autonomous quality that is not to be necessarily tied to print literacy and its
institutions. Apple's recent call for a revisiting of the current model and
structure of Music DRM is important, especially when we take into account the current efforts, at least in Europe, to open up iTunes FairPlay
and to mandate a form of interoperability between it and other formats.
And, according to a Jupiter Research Study released just days after the
publication of Steve Jobs's essay on music, "62% [of Music Industry execu-
tives] believed that dropping DRM and releasing music files that can be
enjoyed on any MP3 player would boost the take-up of digital music
generally."[10] One can easily explain the failure of eBooks, at least in the
United States, not only because of the difficulty of reading either on the
screen or on specialized readers, but also because of the insistence on relatively stringent DRM. In France, to take another example, the situation is
radically different, thanks in large part to the implementation of the book-
selling business in cities and the role played by bookstores.[11] Publishers and
bookstores were, until very recently, close collaborators, but with the promise of digital books and the threat it represents to the traditional bookstore
model, a divide has emerged. On the one hand, publishers appear to be determined to exploit DRM eBooks (it is not clear in what format yet), thus
directly competing with their former allies. On the other hand, bookstores, in their majority, perceive the digital book as, inevitably, a "dématé-
rialisation"[12] of the book, for some fatally threatening their livelihood. In
both cases, however, we encounter something familiar: the unwillingness
to modify business models in order to adapt to and to take advantage of the
digital environment.[13] While publishers are wary of the large (and mostly
American) online sellers, bookstores have not been imaginative in exploiting opportunities offered by the digital environment.

   The digital marketplace will virtualize the book and not dematerialize
it: it will do so in part because of the modification in reading habits and
their function in the marketplace. The digital market place is a natural
extension of the emerging digital literacy, and traditional producers and
distributors of printed intellectual property need, for their own survival,
to accept its reality and its consequences. Much like the entertainment

industry, new business and distribution models are required, models that, for their success, have to take into account the practices put into place by digital culture and the nature of the digital object. Virtuality, in this case, is part and parcel of the materiality of the digital environment. The virtual nature of the digital book does not necessarily imply the death of the bookstore or the disappearance of the book as a cultural object. It does mean a change in the way bookstores conduct their business, a change that, at least in some European countries, will also have an impact on the urban scene. In a revealing manner, the difficulties faced by both publishers and bookstores reflect the importance of digital literacy and the ways in which it radically challenges the established models of authorship and authors' associated rights, as well as the institutions, legal and financial, that they have made possible.

It is perhaps useful to recall, in this case, another effort at providing a flexible Music DRM, one that did not meet any success. The reason to discuss it lies not so much in its failure to garner either industry or popular support, but instead in the social model it tried to put forward. The format is called Light Weight Digital Rights Management (LWDRM) and is proposed by the Fraunhofer Institute and the creators of MP3. It is meant to take into account the current norms prevalent in the online culture and to provide a flexible control over copyrighted material:

Based on personalization instead of copy protection, LWDRM offers a reasonable balance of security on the on hand and user-friendly handling of content on the other hand. The basic idea is to allow fair use and private copying if the consumer is willing to mark the content with his identity by applying his personal digital signature, thus accepting the responsibility not to use the content in a way that is considered infringing. The concept of accepting responsibility by applying a signature has been common and accepted practice in the area of print media for years, and has been adapted for the handling of audiovisual content. Depending on the prevalent legislation, consumers can transfer content to portable devices or share them with family members and friends. In case of public dissemination through open file sharing systems or websites, however, content can be traced back to the consumer.[14]

The criticisms of LWDRM center on the viability of the proposed DRM technology (what is normally referred to as Mark and Trace, i.e., the watermarking of the digital object and its trail on the network) and on some of its practical and technical shortcomings.

Without entering into a technical discussion of the merits of the model, I would like to point out some interesting features of the proposal, features that may still be relevant for future models of rights management. First, in order for the technology to work, it requires a digital identity and a digital signature. Second, it is also flexible enough that it can be adapted to accommodate local laws and customs. As such it is promising because it is one of the few proposals that, at least in principle, invokes a concept of responsibility that is, initially, pragmatic (signature and associated responsibility) while allowing for a somewhat flexible DRM model. Furthermore, it tries to take into account normal uses and patterns of copying and sharing (something that Apple's iTunes Music Store and iPod try to do as well). In other words, LWDRM, despite its deficiencies, points to the role to be played by an expanded form of digital identity in the management of digital rights, a management that is no longer restricted to the protection of copyright, but one that takes into account the differences introduced by the digital environment and thus recognizes new rights to users. Furthermore, it tries to address the complex jurisdictional issue by moving away from a universal model for rights and their management and recognizing the importance of national and cultural dimensions of intellectual property laws and traditions. LWDRM is at the intersection of emerging technological implementations at a large scale of digital identity and the current copyright and intellectual property debates. Its relevance lies in the recognition of users' rights and the ensuing shift from simply the need for a Digital Rights Management solution to a technology and a social contract, or something resembling it, that takes into account the need for digital rights in terms of digital culture and its environment and not only with a view to preserving and propagating rights inherited from print culture. Ultimately, it is an early and tentative recognition of digital literacy and its reality. Digital rights are essential for future development because they put into play the need to reflect on new models of exchange and transmission of digital objects (in this instance, digital music files) that will rely on digital identity and its associated features and components as well as on new business models for entities involved in the creation, distribution, and sale of digital objects (music, videos, etc.). At this point in time, it is clear that we lack the infrastructure as well as sufficient penetration of technology for such a proposal (or a more sophisticated and flexible variation) to be realistic.

The divide between print and digital does not necessarily have to be a conflict between two literacies. The current culture wars focusing on copyright and intellectual property are in effect a struggle over the future of digital literacy and its economic consequences and potentially new business models. It is ironic that print and the publishing industry owe much of their success to the early history of the technology and its dissident if not revolutionary use, whereas currently they have become the representatives of the authorities they once helped challenge and neutralize. If, as it is often argued, the rise of print culture and the success of the book as a cultural object were tied to the Reformation, then perhaps what is needed nowadays is a digital reformation, one that will be able to encourage digital literacy in its quest for new cultural horizons.

This initial divide echoes or, even better, encapsulates the multiplicity of divides our society faces as we integrate more technologies into every aspect of daily life. But it also affords us a unique perspective for evaluating the historical dimension of the new technologies and the intellectual frameworks that make the digital environment coherent, cohesive, and intelligible. In other words, the complex relations between the print and the digital are symptomatic of a wider, more far-reaching constellation of issues that call for a new literacy and new cultural practices and norms. But even this brief survey invites us to think in more detail and precision about the digital object in all its diversity and complexity.[15]

A key difference introduced by digital literacy lies in the emergence of new rights associated with the practices made possible by the digital environment, practices that, in their nature, are in some significant ways in conflict with those of the once predominant print culture. If print and its culture led to the legal institutionalization of authorship and its associated rights, digital culture is leading, in turn, to the recognition of rights that are those of users who can be at one and the same time, thanks to the technology, authors and readers, editors and distributors. DRM is essentially the technological implementation of the association of rights and privileges with content, and digital rights are, on the other hand, the association of uses with the digital object. A significant recognition of digital literacy, within the context of DRM and hacking and "piracy," was expressed by the U.S. Second Circuit Court in the section of its decision in the case of *Universal City Studios v. Corley*, when it formulated its opinion about "code as speech."[16] The decision is revealing, from our perspective, because of the role played by readability in the recognition of text as speech and thus potentially granting it constitutional protections. The text is worth citing at length:

> Communication does not lose constitutional protection as "speech" simply because it is expressed in the language of computer code. Mathematical formulae and musical scores are written in "code," that is, symbolic notations not comprehensible to the uninitiated, and yet both are covered by the First Amendment. If someone chose to write a novel entirely in computer object code by using strings of 1's and 0's for each letter of each word, the resulting work would be no different for constitutional purposes than if it had been written in English. The "object code" version would be incomprehensible to readers outside the programming community (and tedious to read even for most within the community), but it would be no more incomprehensible than a work written in Sanskrit for those unversed in that language. The undisputed evidence reveals that even pure object code can be, and often is, read and understood by experienced programmers. And source code (in any of its various levels of complexity) can be read by many more. Ultimately, however, the ease with which a work is comprehended is irrelevant to the constitutional inquiry. If computer code is distinguishable from conventional speech for First Amendment purposes, it is not because it is written in an obscure language.
>
> Of course, computer code is not likely to be the language in which a work of literature is written.[17] Instead, it is primarily the language for programs executable by a computer. These programs are essentially instructions to a computer.

The court recognizes the specialized nature of computer programming but also its accessibility, as text and discourse, to a large public. It also points to the existence of a community, and for our purposes here, a learned community, that can read and evaluate such code in all its manifestations, from "source" to "object." In other words, the test for deciding the status of the language (and I would say the discourse) that constitutes a program in its various stages relies on the existence and the perpetuation of a group of readers who are also authors, a group of programmers who are, from the court's point of view, learned (and literate) readers. In fact, for some, writing code is explicitly a literary activity: "Literate programming is a programming methodology that combines a programming language with a documentation language, making programs more robust, more portable, and more easily maintained than programs written only in a high-level language. Computer programmers already know both kinds of languages; they need only learn a few conventions about alternating between languages to create programs that are works of *literature*. A literate programmer is an *essayist* who writes programs for humans to understand, instead of primarily writing instructions for machines to follow."[18] If the court singles out comprehension and readability as criteria for recognizing the literate status of code, the programmer, on the other hand, goes further. For him, programming is akin to the essay, and whose primary audience is the community of programmers. In other words, programming is a new form of authorship that produces both computer instructions and a discourse for others to read, interpret, and modify. It is an authorship that shapes to some degree the user's interaction with the digital environment but that is also a visible and readable essay that can display, in most cases, its archive and archeology to the initiated or the interested. If we were to compare it to the manuscript, programming (unless the source code is not released) is a digital document that is both the final product and the effort that produces it: it is an open, unfinished manuscript that can be inspected at the source, so to speak, and at the moment of encounter with its "finished" manifestation. Literate programming, as described by Knuth, is also important because it highlights the significance of literate practices; comments are the equivalent to the ancient *scholias* and the ongoing need to read and reread code makes the case for access and openness. In other words, literate programming, especially with the growth of scripting languages and the increasing popularity of Web interfaces, is fundamentally an inclusive activity. Scripting languages (PHP, Perl, etc.) are important because they have driven the evolution of what has been termed Web 2.0, and thus they have become an integral part of the back end as well as the look and feel of the digital environment.[19] They are also mostly visible and readable, thus allowing for users and surfers to easily adapt some of the code. They collapse, in a sense, the difference between source and object code because they are, for the most part, embedded. They are dynamic, easily adaptable, much like the environment they make possible. They also extend the concept of digital literacy beyond the management of access into new forms of authorship and sharing.

Perhaps the best example of the influence of scripting languages and their evolution in terms of digital literacy is provided by the latest Apple operating system, designated Leopard. Apple offers its users two easy ways to "program" their own widgets, using preset templates and not requiring any prior knowledge of programming or scripting languages. The first, called Web Clip, is simply a polished cut-and-paste operation, from the browser, that will make it possible for users to automate their viewing experience of specific sites. In this fashion, and as its name implies, the Web Clip widget accentuates the growing reliance on the anthological turn and continues the trend of a personalization of the surfing experience, tying together desktop and network and giving the user bigger control over the look and feel of his online experience as well as the choice of what to see and to read. The second component, more powerful but relatively easy to use, is called Dashcode. While it is for power users, Apple describes it as follows: "Ever wish you could make your very own Dashboard widget? Say hello to Dashcode. With it, you can get a widget up and running in minutes, even if you've never written a line of code in your life. Choose from a handful of Dashcode widget templates—including a countdown timer, RSS feed, photocast, podcast, or gauge—or create a widget from scratch with a blank template. Drag in an RSS link and your widget populates with a full feed."[20] The digital environment, now relying on the fundamental changes in the operating system brought about by the new practices popularized by digital culture, invites readers and surfers to become active participants: it gives them the opportunity to become authors and for some at least, programmers.

In this case, digital literacy, both personal and collective, both signed and anonymous, encourages readers to become coders and programmers, and ultimately, digital authors. It functions, in a way, as a digital learning environment where beginners and specialists have, in principle, the same access. In short, it is an essay in digital conversion.[21]

III. Digital Literacy and the Anthological Turn

But digital literacy goes well beyond the validation of new and different rights: it has its own literate structure. A significant dimension, and one that has become perhaps the most popular and the most debated of the current generation of Web presences, is represented by the diverse forms of group publishing or, in some cases, of what is best described as collective generation of content. Wikipedia is perhaps the most well-known instance of such tools, due to its remarkable success and to the various controversies it has generated, focusing mostly on the reliability and validity of some of its content and its comparisons to the more conventional sources of collected knowledge, normally authored by specialists.[22] Wikipedia is the heir of a long tradition of encyclopedic works from the Middle Ages to the Early Modern period, and to the *Encyclopédie* of D'Alembert and Diderot, and finally to their more modern variations. But Wikipedia, much like other similar tools that allow for distributed and constantly changing models for authorship and publication, is, in my opinion, fundamentally different precisely because of its production model. In this respect, and despite its specificity (predominantly textual and relatively anonymous, topic or subject oriented and organized, different versions available in different languages thus marking cultural specificities, etc.), it is still characterized by what I call an assembly model of authorship. Wikipedia, curiously enough and because of its ideological commitment to the wisdom of crowds, functions as an anonymizer and points to the complex politics of authorship in the digital age, especially within the context of the emergence of a de facto reference that is often used without any discrimination. Such politics are most visible within the polemics surrounding the content of Wikipedia as a conflictual space (and this can relate to an article covering a standard, a historically disputed event or an individual) that is often presented (mostly by the press) as a process whose defining principle is to harmonize content and knowledge over the long term and to eventually produce an acceptable consensus. The repeated debates concerning the validity of Wikipedia entries have centered mostly on the role and function of editorial monitoring and interventions. But well beyond the desire to tie credibility to the editorial function, the current structure of Wikipedia and its derivatives embody the dynamic nature of knowledge (or at least its popular manifestation) as open-ended, as a work in progress, as an infinite exercise. In a sense, the structure of the Wiki itself, an always editable and fully archived platform, mirrors both the collection and the transformation of accessible information into more usable and reusable fragments. But what are the long-term implications of such a condition of information sharing and knowledge production propelled by the popularity of Wikipedia? Without wishing to provide any answers, I think it is important to note, in this respect, that despite the continuing growth and popularity of Wikipedia, the nascent projects of WikiBooks and similar undertakings have met limited success. This is most informative, as it shows that every time a successful digital tool tries to mimic and compete with a conventional fixed object (in this instance the book) it somewhat fails. How do we account for this divergence? It seems to me that it is precisely the anthological nature of the encyclopedic dimension of Wikipedia that accounts to a large degree for its success and popularity, not only because it provides easy and rapid access to a wealth of information but because this anthological dimension is constitutive of both digital literacy and its unique forms of authorship and readership.

The use of Wikis is of course not limited to Wikipedia and its imitators. It has also begun to be accepted within large corporate networks for the purpose of managing complex projects that require continuous sharing and review of information. Furthermore, it is being tested for scientific publishing and consultation of large databases. A recent example, experimental at the time of writing this chapter, is WikiProfessional.[23] It collects already available information from a number of professional databases and then will allow access, authorship, and annotation to specialists. In other words, it provides already published material and exploits the Wiki technology in order to make it possible to annotate and share new discoveries or modifications to established norms. Thus, WikiProfessional is more suited to an active research community, and its tailoring of the open authorship function of the original Wiki reflects the need and the desire to have a more credible and reliable format and forum for the digital production and transmission of viable knowledge. Information published on the Wiki is also semantically tagged, thus allowing for a sophisticated access to it, marked by both a personal as much as a collective categorization.

The assembly model of authorship is perhaps most visible in other popular Web tools, such as Flickr and Del.icio.us, to name only a few. It is an assembly in the sense of a collection, a grouping that is both defined by an initial selection and that is also open to modification and adaptation. Ultimately, then, the assembly model produces an anthology that is tailored to the current tools, content, and taste. It is this anthological turn that I would like to discuss briefly in this section in order to highlight both the literary dimension of many of the digital norms currently in vogue and that are shaping both the technological development and the economic models underlying the deployment of the latest generation of large-scale Web hubs. Whether initially put together by a single individual or researcher or by a group of disparate readers, the anthological model makes it possible to transform and present collected items in a dynamic and open publication of potentially new knowledge. This anthological sharing is, in my opinion, a surreptitious selection and dissemination of apparently unrelated snippets or fragments into meaningful collections where meaning is largely derived from an association of content, instead of a meaning necessarily tied with authors and their identity or intent. Meaning is often derived from flexible categorization (or tagging).

While anthologies, at least in their classical forms, were always sites for the expression of individual tastes and opinions reflected by the organization, order, and selection of assembled fragments as well as the use of commonly available and shared sources, the digital anthological practice accentuates the inherent tendency of the anthology to minimize if not collapse the differences between authors and readers. If the anthology silently marks the "incestuous" links between readership and authorship, the digital anthological phenomenon celebrates the unbound potential for reading to modify, manipulate, redefine, and appropriate content. But, in this instance, both authorship and reading have been, if not reinvented, at least displaced and remodeled. First, the new anthological turn has been extended to new media, most notably images and videos, thus allowing for a more complex interaction with content that in the past had kept the

reader or the spectator at a distance or, in some ways, in a relatively passive position. The growing complexity of interaction between users and
the digital environment illustrated by the anthological turn has currently
been transformed by the success of a new tool that was first launched as a
brief presence-management format, one that exemplifies the anthological
and polyphonic dimension of online digital identity. Twitter represents, if
its current evolution is sustained, a potential blueprint for a path that leads
from an initial simple communication tool to a large-scale platform for
presence management, one that can ultimately shape new social practices.
Twitter is unique in that it restricts the amount of communication while
allowing for a broad sharing of exchanges derived from a variety of sources.
In this respect, it stands out as the first second-generation tool that exclusively relies on the flexibility of the digital object: its relatively small size
when it is limited to expressing a timely individual option and the ease
of its aggregation. Thus, the anthological turn, continuously evolving,
becomes a key to a form of social density within a distributed knowledge-
sharing platform.[24] The current anthological practice is immensely successful owing to the ways in which it exploits the interface between the
technological (easy access, authoring tools, tagging, etc.) and an individualistic drive to distinction. It also illustrates some of the literate features
of the new digital literacy and the ways in which it recuperates and appro-
priates print culture models.

IV. Digital Civil Wars

The second case of a digital divide is perhaps more subtle but no less important: I define it for our purposes as the growing gap between the speed
and complexity of technological development and the thresholds of usability and access. While new tools, systems, and applications are often (if not
always) sold and marketed as delivering an improved and especially simplified ease of use, we all know from our experience and from the success
of what is best termed the Digital Support Industry, that they are instead
more complex and can be much more difficult to manage and to maintain.
This divide is significant for a number of reasons. First, because the path
of its evolution has created a new class, a new aristocracy of the digital age:
the nerd or geek culture has been elevated to produce a new intelligentsia,

and they are the technocrats of our information and knowledge societies. And this development extends well beyond the current generational gap of the young who are assumed to know how to use computers and the elderly who do not. Second, the growing complexity of the digital environment has privacy and security implications.

The complexity creates a new de facto set of "social classes," those who are users and those who are manipulators. Users tend to be overall more passive, more likely not to modify their digital environment or to feel fully at ease or in control of all the tools they have available at hand. They tend to be, from the perspective of the "manipulator," underachievers, for they do not fully exploit the potential of the technologies they have at hand. In a way, they are the followers who, while adopting and adapting to new tools, tend to remain more comfortable with a restricted version of the digital environment. But what is important, from our perspective, is the fact that a different form of literacy characterizes users and manipulators. On the one hand, we have users who are tentative or unsure of themselves and who tend to encounter problems they are unable to resolve on their own. And on the other, the "manipulators" are in some ways the creators of the new environment; they are the new "authors," the ones whose level of proficiency allows them not only to receive but also to publish, in the digital sense of the term. The "manipulators" are the élite of the new digital learned communities. Thus, digital literacy points the way for a representation of the current state of digital culture but, equally, it provides us with a model for evaluating policies meant for bridging the digital divide so often lamented by the politicians.

In order to illustrate a case in which this hierarchy in digital literacy plays out in the real world, let us begin with a simple example. Browsers used to be relatively benign and straightforward tools. They are perhaps the most familiar components of the digital environments. But with the new technologies and the fragmentation of, as well as the emergence of, digital identity (we will return to this issue shortly), browsers have become, among other things, the primary space of what is best described as digital civil wars. Browsers have become the privileged site of the new digital literacy in all of its density, ranging from managing security and privacy to negotiating with the new discursive practices and the new competencies they require. Browsers continue to shape users' experiences and expectations within the digital environment, and they frame the perspectives informing the valuation of access, transmission, and reproduction of information.

The phenomenal rise in identity theft, in security breaches that jeopardize private information of large groups, the ongoing onslaught of spam in mailboxes, are but a sign of this digital civil war. It is a conflict between the open and often experimental nature of the network and the desire, by a determined minority, to exploit it. But beyond such a configuration, the growing importance of the digital environment makes its security a priority because it increasingly involves matters and transactions that used to be reserved to more "trusted" forms of exchange. While the security problems are complex and multifaceted, they also highlight the importance of digital literacy as well as the need for new contracts between users and providers, between users and software makers. Currently, providers and software makers, while they are allowed to have restrictive licenses and EULAs (End User Licensing Agreements)for their products, they are not held liable for some vulnerabilities or damage caused by their software. In a way, we are still, at the heart of the digital environment, in a one-way-street type of intellectual property model. Users have to agree to a license but sellers have no responsibility. Whereas this model may have been acceptable in the early phases of the digital age, it has become increasingly clear that it needs to be revisited. While no one will argue that secure code is achievable, it is fair to expect relatively secure code and applications and platforms that do not ship with known and fixable vulnerabilities.[25] The growth of the computer security industry testifies to the importance and scale of the problem. Furthermore, it is somewhat perverse to find some of the major purveyors of OS (operating systems) and other major applications become security software providers.[26] This trend extends in part the initial model behind licensing by focusing responsibility on the user and excluding, at least in legal terms, the provider from any responsibility.

The minor detour into computer security provides a better context for the changes in the status of the browser, especially from a security perspective. Browsers are now a magnet for virus and worm writers, for phishers and identity thieves. Phishing is a trap of resemblance: it relies on seemingly official but in fact fake e-mails whose purpose is to lure users to

Web sites where they may disclose their private or financial information to a scammer. Phishing deploys a set of familiar and coordinated technologies: e-mail, browsers, and secure login. But it also relies on the persuasive powers of appearance: the fake site has to look like a legitimate one, and the users are expected to encounter a number of recognizable elements and features. Thus, in this instance, the design and the color schemes play an equally important role as the e-mails that initiate the phishing lure. In both instances, the user has to be a careful reader in order to avoid falling into the trap of resemblance. Browsing is no longer simply a reading activity restricted to textual content; it now calls for an informed vigilance on the part of the computer user that requires the coordination between content and form in order to evaluate and establish the legitimacy of a message or a site.

But phishing is also interesting because it is currently the most widespread form of social engineering crime and as such allows for an examination of some of the intricacies involving digital identity, privacy, and security within the digital environment as well as the role played by the User Interface in potentially facilitating its exploitation. It also reflects some of the difficulties attendant to the slow movement of financial or private transactions into a fully networked environment that relies on the Web as an interface and that requires an increasingly sophisticated literacy on the part of users. Phishing, by exploiting the confusion made possible by resemblance between the authentic and the fake, points to density of appearance and user interfaces within the digital environment and their relations to security and ultimately trust. It also makes it clear that users and Web surfers run serious risks even when visiting what in principle ought to be secure and trustworthy sites. As reported by a *Wired* magazine blog, the U.S. Transportation Security Agency (TSA) Traveler Identity Site appeared to be a victim of a successful phishing attack due to bad or clumsy redirection of site traffic and management of layout and content: "All indications are yes, and that a malicious phishing attack has been launched against travelers who have or think they have been delayed because they are on a watchlist or have a name similar to a person on the watchlist. A new link on the TSA's Our Travelers page directs people who 'were told you are on a Federal Government Watch List' to click on a link taking them to this site, which, by all accounts, fits the profile of an attempt to harvest personal information and identity document details."[27] This initial reaction by Web observers led the TSA to modify its page and to have it redirect to a TSA domain, thus avoiding the appearance of phishing. It remains true, however, that the mere redirection to a different domain, especially on a sensitive site such as the TSA, raises legitimate concerns and illustrates the prevalence and complexity of phishing. The site redirects to a http://ms.desyne.com domain, thus raising concerns about its legitimacy and its relations to TSA. Other details discussed by *Wired* journalists show how easy it is, in the current computer security environment, to suspect even legitimate sites, owing to the role played by look and feel factors and by trust grounded in expectations based on a history of browsing. Ultimately, this example demonstrates the significance of a digital literacy, both for users and surfers and for programmers and site designers.

In this particular instance, just for an example, the mismatch between the two domains (tsa.gov and ms.desyne.com) and the absence of a secure HTTP connection (normally signaled by the initials https and accompanied by an icon representing a lock or a similar image conveying the idea of a secure transaction) are enough to raise the suspicion of a vigilant visitor. While phishing relies on a trap of similarity for its success, it also points to the crucial role played by elements of the interface that normalize the user's experience and that have become an integral part of online life.

But issues raised by computer security in all of its aspects go well beyond the problem of identity theft illustrated by phishing: they also indicate an evolution, within the technological community, of the abstractions at work in representing the agents and variables at play in the digital environment. Such a shift is embodied by a theory (some would say it is a marketing tool) known as the holistic security approach. In this scheme, the best defense in the current computer security conditions is a total approach, an attitude and a set of tools that take into account all of the available variables when it comes to assessing security, from the operating system, to the applications and the network and, ultimately the user.[28] In this version of what I am calling the Digital Civil Wars, the key term is convergence: convergence of tools and threats, convergence of emerging technologies and practices and unknown security risks, and, ultimately, convergence between digital literacy and the management of computer presence and its associated risks. In a sense, this model is a double-edged sword: on the one hand, it shifts some of the responsibility away from hardware and software producers to users, thus emphasizing the importance of increased digital literacy and, on the other, it recognizes the nature of security threat and the impossibility of a clear solution or closure. While security experts differ in their evaluation of the viability of such an approach to security, I would like to focus on the cultural and discursive assumptions underlying such abstractions and their relevance to some of the issues I raised in the Introduction.

The holistic approach signals a shift in the perception of the relations between users and their computers or, more precisely, a change in the nature of the interactions between individuals and groups and the digital environment. From the stance of a holistic approach, the digital environment in its entirety (we might say in its virtuality) is seen and thought of as a body, a body that is constituted by physical and virtual elements, but a body nonetheless. Furthermore, this body is in essence an extension, in digital terms, of the body of either an individual or a collectivity. In other words, we have here, and within the context of risk management and security, the actualization of a posthuman form of corporeality that is not exclusively virtual or imaginary, since it has real and concrete effects. The holistic approach transfers the hybrid condition from the integration of mechanical or electronic parts to the human body into the extension of human bodily features and characteristics into the digital environment itself. Thus, the responsibility of the user is represented in terms of an individualized form of health care that requires ever-increased vigilance, but one that also represents threats in terms of a struggle for health.[29] It also *naturalizes* the security problems haunting the digital environment. Thus, we move into a world where modified natural models shape and inform our modes of being within the virtualities of digital culture. Whatever the merits of such a model may be, it remains that security problems, while being the result of the convergence of new technologies and their unknown risks, are also the ingredients for an increased management of the digital environment, one that relies on digital literacy but one that also risks curtailing its potential. Convergence implies also heightened controls and even censorship in order to ensure the integrity and security of either sensitive or valuable information. And it is precisely in this fashion that the apparent weakness of digital tools can become a new and lucrative business opportunity.

From an institutional perspective, it would seem that a secure environment is necessarily a managed environment. In other words, security can only be obtained by a constant surveillance, if not the curtailing, of some online activities. While such an approach may be acceptable in some corporate networks, it raises serious privacy concerns. Once more we encounter the inevitable association of digital presence and its intimate ties to digital identity and literacy with digital rights. Rights have become associated with, if not a feature of presence, a digital presence. And presence, in the digital environment, much like digital identity itself, is fundamentally multiple and polyphonic. The problems raised by the current state of computer security and their association with redefined and expanded notions of national security are but an indication of the essentially political dimension of the issues we are discussing.

V. Digital Citizenship and the Politics of Digital Identity

The physiological or biological model of computer security is certainly not a new figure; it has its root in a rather all-too-common representation of historical change and evolution, and we find it in classical texts as well as theological writings. The correspondence between the different stages of the normal life of an individual and that of a group, a nation, or an empire has been used to explain the rise and fall of states and, among other things, the evolution of science and the advancement of knowledge. It can provide a familiar way to explain change but also a useful reference for dealing with innovation.[30] The return to the individual as a measure for the digital is nonetheless deceiving, since in this context the individual is rather radically transformed and tied to a modified sense of place and forms of presence. And along with these modified concepts, a set of elementary notions are to be redefined if not reinvented and reimagined. From property to ownership, from nationality and identity to responsibility and its jurisdictional limits, we are faced with challenges to some of the most basic assumptions concerning our ways of belonging to groups and to society and our culture. In order to illustrate some of the implications of this reimagined version of ourselves within the new and at times uncharted territory of the digital, I shall discuss a few representative features of digital identity.

Digital identity, as mentioned earlier, is fundamentally polyphonic (multiple and diverse, allowing for more flexibility and pseudo-anonymity). It is a function, in part, of the ways in which it is deployed, acknowledged, recognized, and, ultimately, authenticated. Thus:[31]

(a) it spans jurisdiction: the same identity or its multiple manifestations or iterations can be deployed in different if not competing jurisdictions for different purposes.

(b) it is not necessarily tied to a place or a particular genealogy. Unlike "documentary" identity, digital ID requires a presence but is not, strictly speaking, a function of an "origin."

(c) Digital ID is the result of an aggregation. It is constructed, over time, by the profile created from the history of its activities and movements. The implications of this shift towards an aggregate conception (and accountability) of identity are determining for privacy because they imply the separation between the identity's history and its owner and the surrogate control of the profile by third parties (government, private corporations, etc.).

Obviously, digital identity is not restricted to the features listed above. I chose to emphasize them because, for the purposes of our discussion in this chapter, they allow us to easily identify key issues and to recognize some of the difficulties raised by the slow transition to digital identity. While the transition to digital identity is still in its early stages, its polyphonic nature has given rise to a set of paradoxes, if not at times contradictions, for users as much as for legislators and regulators, and ultimately for politicians and for national governments. These paradoxes center on a number of major issues: management of identity and presence in an increasingly complex digital environment; the need for a new understanding of digital privacy that takes into account the potential as well as the dangers of digital identity; the emerging jurisdictional conflict between regional and national authorities with the absence of harmonious (if such is ever possible) rules to manage jurisdictional differences; and ultimately, the growing importance of available personal data and the increased pressure to collect and store it, and the rules for managing such stored managed personal data. Fundamentally, digital identity, by modifying the mechanics of the relations between citizens and their governments (i.e., the nature of exchanging and obtaining legitimate identity-related data and its symbolic power), changes also the nature of the relation between citizens and their respective governments. Before examining some concrete examples of these changes, it is useful to formulate some broad questions pertaining to the interaction between the complex world of technology and digital culture and what we might term "rights." The transition to the digital, as we have seen even in our brief discussion of the shift from print to the current environment, entails a redefinition of key abstractions that are essentially of a cultural nature and that receive, in different contexts, diverse political and legal formulations: digital presence and individual responsibility; protected rights and obligations; access to information, its manipulation, and the associated forms of ownership and permissions to transmit and exchange such information; the right to anonymity within the new digital environment; relations between the transactional nature of the digital environment and privacy and the growing tendency to collect, store, and analyze personal data; and, ultimately, the desire to create a managed form of digital identity based on some secure system, like biometrics. Digital identity raises the thorny question of the relations between sovereignty and network-based jurisdictions.

The case brought by LICRA against Yahoo! in France is an excellent example of the complexities of the jurisdictional politics of the networked digital environment and the ensuing difficulties for harmonizing different if not conflicting cultural norms about sensitive topics such as racism and freedom of speech. LICRA based its argument on French law and on its prohibition of the display of Nazi emblems and symbols. While this prohibition is explicitly inscribed in Article R645–1 of the French Civil Code, and thus applies in all French territory, Yahoo! is an American company that hosts servers distributed worldwide. In other words, the case, at least from our perspective here, centers on the question of nationality and a sense of place, within the frontiers of the digital environment. It raises further the unresolved question of the applicability of a national law to an entity or a digital presence that is neither restricted to national borders nor limited to a single jurisdiction. But beyond these initial questions, the case pointed to the intertwining of legal and cultural decisions and norms and their technical implications; for if Yahoo! is required to make sure that French citizens, within national French territory, do not gain access to Nazi memorabilia, technically, such a decision implies the removal of all such items from Yahoo!'s network and thus amounts, to some legal analysts in the United States at least, to the application of a French law in the United States, a law that contradicts American Freedom of Speech protections, even for racist organizations.[32] What we have here is a clash of legal traditions over the limits of freedom of expression marked by history and culture; What is protected and under what circumstances? What constitutes expression and, especially, what constitutes responsibility, especially in a networked environment? It puts into relief the conflict between national jurisdictions and highlights the ambiguous and problematic status of digital technology. The digital environment critically modifies the key abstractions at the core of the formulations of some national laws. The case illustrates the difficulties that some have termed the "offline" world and governments' efforts to regulate the digital environment. For us, it represents another significant case in which the concept of digital literacy is crucial, for literacy applies to all aspects of a culture, from reading to law, from politics to identity.

But this jurisdictional breakdown, which at times makes for unresolved conflicts between nations and governments, gives rise also to a drive to formulate new forms of government-controlled identity that are primarily digital and that are ultimately aimed at regaining and strengthening national controls over digital identity, or at least over the freedom to surf the digital environment. For the first example, we can look at the United Kingdom's proposed scheme for a secure national identity system and its implications for privacy and for the required infrastructure for deploying such a large-scale system. Second, we can examine the digital censorship put into place, on a national level, by countries like China and Saudi Arabia.

According to the *OpenNet Initiative*, a collaborative academic entity bringing together research centers at four universities,[33] "China has earned the dubious distinction as the world leader in filtering Internet content. The Chinese state-run Internet censoring system is without parallel, both in the technical sophistication of the filtering apparatus and in the breadth of topics subject to blocking. This *OpenNet Initiative* Bulletin describes recent additions to Chinese law that strengthen the legal and administrative basis for the Internet regulatory system."[34] The summary statement suffices to point out the potential limitation of the freedoms made possible by the digital environment and the controls that can be introduced by national governments in order to manage extensive censorship and/or surveillance of their citizens. While it is always possible to find technological detours around the censorship/filtering systems, such solutions tend to be accessible to a very small number of savvy users. In other words, national governments can, if they are willing to invest the required resources, implement a draconian form of censorship that is far more effective than the old-fashioned, offline version. Countries can control not only access to otherwise openly available information; they can also redirect traffic to sites where they have full control over content and where they can track and store users' habits and movements online.[35] While China tends to base its filtering and censorship model on political factors, Saudi Arabia has other concerns. According to the *OpenNet Initiative*, the Saudis present an altogether different model from the Chinese. Their concerns appear to be primarily religious and ethical, and, surprisingly, much less political:

> The *OpenNet Initiative* (ONI) has tested filtering in Saudi Arabia over a three-year period. We found that the Kingdom's filtering focuses on a few types of content: pornography (98% of these sites tested blocked in our research), drugs (86%), gambling (93%), religious conversion, and sites with tools to circumvent filters (41%). In contrast, Saudi Arabia shows less interest in sites on gay and lesbian issues (11%), politics (3%), Israel (2%), religion (less than 1%), and alcohol (only 1 site). Unlike filtering in states such as China, the policies, procedures, and philosophy for Saudi Arabia's filtering system are relatively transparent and documented on the Web site of its Internet Services Unit (ISU). Users who try to access forbidden sites see a Web page informing them that the site is prohibited. Despite this openness about filtering, the system inevitably errs, resulting in overblocking of unrelated content.[36]

The differences between the two countries and their policies give us almost the full range of online censorship and surveillance on a national scale. On the one hand, an extensive and secretive set of policies that exclude the citizen from the most minimal information as to what is being blocked and why, and, on the other, a relatively transparent policy that allows users and citizens to request policy changes. But what may be most informative about both policies are the changes in the ways in which national authorities, for whatever reasons, can shape their citizens' experiences within the digital environment. As an example of the limitations of such extensive filtering systems (what the *OpenNet Initiative* calls "errors"), we can point out the Saudi heightened sensitivity to religious conversion resulting in the blockage of a variety of sites that deal with scientific aspects of conversion, let alone other variants. Overblocking reflects the contradictions between the technological dimension of filtering (filters based on keywords and that cannot take into account ambiguity) and the complexity of representing accurately, across cultures and disciplines, the semantic density of a word.

While these two cases represent some of the more visible instances of national efforts to manage citizens' digital experience, other, more surreptitious forms of censorship have, unfortunately, become all too common. These result from political pressures applied by powerful national governments on online service providers, mostly search engines, in order to force them to remove "undesirable" information from their archives. This is most evident in the case of China, which has not hesitated to threaten denying access to large companies if they did not agree to some of its censorship-related requests. But the most dangerous dimension of this equation lies in the acceptance of self-censorship by Western companies in order to gain access to the promised land of the Chinese market. This was clearly expressed by Google's representative, Elliot Schrage, in his testimony before the Committee on International Relations:

> I'm here today to answer any and all questions you might have about how we are attempting to do business in China. I certainly don't—my colleagues certainly don't—expect everyone to agree with our decision to launch a new service inside this challenging, complex, promising market. I hope my testimony will help explain how we came to our decision, what we're seeking to accomplish, and how we're seeking to accomplish it. . . . At the outset, I want to acknowledge what I hope is obvious: Figuring out how to deal with China has been a difficult

exercise for Google. The requirements of doing business in China include self-censorship—something that runs counter to Google's most basic values and commitments as a company. Despite that, we made a decision to launch a new product for China—Google.cn—that respects the content restrictions imposed by Chinese laws and regulations. Understandably, many are puzzled or upset by our decision. But our decision was based on a judgment that Google.cn will make a meaningful—though imperfect—contribution to the overall expansion of access to information in China.[37]

Google's spokesperson articulates here the classic explanation for self-censorship; access to the Chinese market will make it possible to modify its conditions, from the inside, and hopefully, change its attitudes about freedom of access and censorship of Internet content. What it does not say is that the financial dimension of the Chinese market plays a crucial role in making companies like Google, Yahoo!, and Microsoft, to name only a few, adapt their policies in order to accept conditions that would be rejected elsewhere. While the economic stakes are high, it is also important to ensure that dangerous precedents do not become the norm in curtailing the essential freedoms brought about by the digital environment. Political manifestations of digital identity can be relatively easily curtailed by countries and by service providers willing to compromise principles in order to gain access to large and growing markets. These compromises, as we shall see in Chapter 4, also have serious consequences for the accuracy and integrity of digital archives. But in the last analysis, digital censorship curtails digital literacy: it seeks to limit its potential and to control it. And as we have seen in the case of Digital Rights Management, digital literacy is first and foremost about rights, about digital rights. In a similar fashion, the new digital rights associated not only with protections but also with the privileges that are part and parcel of the digital environment call for a rethinking of how service providers as well as governments and international organizations deal with the question of digital censorship, beyond the simple respect of boundaries and of territorial sovereignties.

At the other end of the responses to the emerging digital identity lies the United Kingdom's proposal for a national ID card. In this case, we are no longer faced with an effort to limit access to information or to control individuals' interaction with the growing digital environment, but instead we have the effort of a government to put to use some of the digital technologies in order to introduce changes that are both cultural and political.[38] The British Home Office describes thus its proposed scheme and its benefits: "ID cards will provide legal UK residents, including foreign nationals, with an easy and secure way of proving who they are. ID cards will be linked to their owners by unique biometric identifiers (for example, fingerprints), which mean we will have a much stronger way of protecting people's identities. Background checks will ensure that claimed identities are real and not stolen, and will prevent criminals using multiple identities."[39] The British ID cards will be, if implemented, the first large-scale deployment of biometrics at the national level, and they have raised serious concerns about the viability of such a deployment and the difficulties it raises from the point of view of privacy protections and personal freedoms. The British scheme grew out of a concern for security and thus has its roots in the desire to firmly establish the identity and nationality of residents, which explains the use of biometrics.[40] Biometrics normally refers to automated methods for the recognition of an individual, based, in principle, on unique physiological or behavioral characteristics, such as fingerprints, facial recognition, retina scan, voice, vein, handwriting, or similar variables. What is often forgotten by most when it comes to biometrics is the fact that biometric authentication is fundamentally comparative: it relies on the comparison of a registered and stored sample with a captured one. And, as it was the case with studies for the British national ID proposal, technical difficulties arise immediately when one is thinking of such large scale capture and storage of sensitive data. Even without discussing the social and political implications of a national biometric ID, it is apparent that the collection of comparative data is fraught with errors and risks. Furthermore, as the LSE Identity Project report pointed out, "the proposals are *too complex, technically unsafe, overly prescriptive,* and *lack a foundation of public trust and confidence.* The current proposals miss key opportunities to establish a secure, trusted and cost-effective identity system."[41] We will discuss further the archiving dimension of large-scale biometric systems in Chapter 4, but for our purposes here, it is important to note that, in relation to digital identity, national biometric systems aim to restrict its polyphony and to strengthen its transactional surveillance. Furthermore, it single-handedly redefines digital privacy from a law-enforcement perspective without taking into account other characteristics of digital identity and the digital environment. We can describe such projects as the governmental efforts to digitize human identity in a form that is privacy invasive. For instance, it is not clear how to handle, except with the promise of improved technology, false negatives and false positives, nor is it clear what additional information is to be collected about each individual beyond the selected biometric variable.[42]

On another level, such proposals invite reflection on the relations between digital culture and its potential for representing the human and the individual (and not only the promise of a posthuman). What are the features that are unique, distinct, and that mark and identify an individual? And what are the legitimate political and social uses of such characteristics? How are governments and citizens to negotiate between the assumed or implied trust of the biometric system and their impact on individual and group privacy? What are the jurisdictional concerns raised by such biometric identification systems and what data should be shared between different jurisdictions? Is there any room for a pseudo-anonymous biometric system that will strip some biometric data of its individual identifying features? It is apparent, if one takes such questions seriously, that biometric ID systems define a new trust relationship between citizens and their governments and therefore imply new modalities of interactions between the two, ranging from simple recognition of citizenship and its rights and privileges to conducting elections and distributing benefits.

While some governments, driven by their growing security concerns, are trying to implement a biometric form of digital identity, service providers and other players in the digital environment have also been proposing a variety of schemes to manage the complex requirements of the emerging digital identity. Most schemes were initially designed for convenience: since users tend to have different online identities for various e-mail accounts, or a diversity of services, it made sense to develop what became known as a Single Sign-On platform that allowed users to access a range of services and tools across the network with a single identity and without the repeated need to identify oneself and to authenticate one's digital identity. In other words, recognizing the polyphonic dimension of digital identity, providers proposed schemes for simplifying managing network presence while, at least for some, trying to benefit from such schemes. In these cases, convenience becomes restrictive and, ultimately, most such efforts failed because of users' reluctance to agree to limit themselves to a minimal range of digital identity.[43] Most schemes, at least so far, have relied on a number of foundational concepts and settings: trust relations between authenticating partners or agencies, single-sign-on, and what is generally referred to as federated identity management. These schemes were almost exclusively credentials-based and relied on some private corporate framework.[44] But there are currently some promising tools in development, such as the Shibboleth framework from the Internet2 working group.[45]

As the reader can imagine, federated identity management relies on a set of basic variables: credentials, access controls, the growth of the availability of sensitive material (banking, private directories, etc.) online, and multiple identities (or what I called in earlier notes the polyphonic nature of digital identity, although polyphony is not limited to this dimension of digital identity). Under such circumstances, there is a clear need for a standards-based set of mechanisms for the management of identity information over a network. One of the key advantages of federated identity management is the reduction of the transmission of identity information, thus reducing both risk to privacy and to identity theft and expenses. In a federated scenario, identity information remains resident in its "original" location and the user is allowed access to additional resources and material on the basis of preestablished relations between institutions and access-granting agencies. This, however, highlights the importance of "institutional" identities and can eventually lead to a new digital divide, one based on the difference in access between those who have an institutional identity and those who do not.

Thus, for an example of a federated identity management scenario, two universities can agree to allow their respective populations to share access to the restricted material they have. In this fashion, they can enlarge the material they now have without having to incur additional costs. They also share their users' digital identities and their associated access controls without having to implement additional security and authentication mechanisms. Thus, if University A and University B decided to share access to their rare-book digital material, any University A member is allowed to view University B material without the need for a University B ID or authentication. Instead, the authentication is shared and passed on because of the trust partnership between the two institutions. While this is the simplest scenario, it illustrates some of the advantages of federated identity management as well as some of the infrastructure it requires. It goes without saying that there are increasingly more complex and demanding scenarios where access needs to be more granular based on security factors and time-sensitive access controls. But the net result of the trust partnership is, in principle, access to more material for the user and an extension of the security perimeter of each of the institutions with minimal additional cost.

In these cases, institutional frameworks are meant to protect as much as possible the privacy of their users while allowing them maximum access to material across the network. But in such an environment, identities are issued by governments or companies, or determined by biometric characteristics. They are associated with attributes and preferences that are managed by both users and issuing authorities. To summarize, Federated Network Identity Management offers the following advantages: (a) convenience and access to dynamic offerings; (b) a global standard that is open, interoperable, and decentralized; (c) it can also provide a set of federated privacy safeguards while making room for adaptation to local markets and cultures; and (d) ultimately, it makes it possible to link identity information between accounts without centrally storing personal information. Users can thus control when and how their accounts and attributes are linked and shared between domains. But nevertheless, within this environment, the fact that identities are issued primarily by governments, companies, or determined by biometric characteristics that are managed by similar entities. They are thus inevitably associated with defining characteristics that are managed by both users and the issuing authorities.[46]

In part in response to such scenarios and the reliance on static institutional models for the representation of identity as well as its associated digital rights and presence, there has been a push to develop and implement what is known as a user-centric digital identification system.[47] What is unique about OpenID? First, it allows users to identify themselves, instead of relying on either a government or an institution. But equally important is the model for identification: it is derived from the most common component of the digital environment, the URI,[48] and therefore it is easily recognized by almost all users and provides a known procedure (that is at the center of the digital environment), for establishing digital identity.[49] From our perspective here, OpenID represents an important shift in the deployment of digital identity with potentially far-reaching consequences. First, it binds identity to a form of network presence; thus an individual may choose to link his identity to the URL of a blog, a Wiki, or a site he maintains. Second, it allows for the storage and management of such identity credentials on either a privately managed server or on servers hosted and managed by third parties and other providers. In other words, OpenID is digital through and through; it mirrors users' experiences in the digital environment and offers a familiar format and choices for managing digital identity.[50] But it also relies on the digital competence and literacy of users who have become active participants, whether through social-networking sites and tools or through their own network presence, for the publication and sharing of digital identities. It maintains and extends the decentralized dimension of the network and reduces the reliance on offline authorities. What it promises, ultimately, is the extension of the current trend of Web operating system and its interfaces to the domain of digital identity and its emerging culture. It also preserves the polyphonic nature of digital identity, making it possible for individuals to maintain a diversity of presences within the network, with their own authentication, privileges, and rights.

Digital identity, within such a context, is primarily a political agency. The politics and social dimensions of the digital environment are the subject of our next chapter.

2

Blogging the City

Digital literacy, as we have seen, is at the center of the changes occurring in the digital environment, inviting new forms of authorship and publication tailored toward the convergence of technologies and digital social practices. But digital literacy is also a framework for understanding the historical evolution tied to the emergence of this new literacy that complexifies the concept of a digital divide and invites a critical if not a radical modification of a set of key concepts and abstractions operative in the articulation of social, cultural, and political norms: presence, location, community, identity, and so on. This evolution is perhaps best observed in blogs, if only because their rapid growth and success make them emblematic.

Digital literacy, in its current state, by touching on all the defining abstractions we have discussed, is not only in conflict with print literacy; it is also at the origin of a broader and more significant conflict, one that opposes models of legitimacy and paradigms of credibility, as they are invested with their own norms and practices (one example: traditional journalism and the growing online competition for print and conventional media).[1] But it would be a mistake to limit this conflict of legitimacy and credibility to a description or discussion of who can say what and with what authority. It is also essentially about forms of authority—cultural, social, and political—and the material or, in our case, digital support that makes them possible. In order to illustrate this phenomenon, we shall proceed in this chapter in an alternating fashion, weaving a narrative between historical models and abstractions of the political and its origins and descriptions of technologies, and the practices they produce and their current and potential political usages. For this purpose, I chose a relatively accessible model because it figures prominently in both scholarly literature and popular ideas about the history and the origin of political practices. While the model, in its simplest version, tells a rather straightforward story, a closer examination of its elements reveals the ideological choices and the diverse uses of historical narratives. It is this type of usage in particular that is revealing, especially when it comes to understanding the current evolution of the emerging practices in the digital environment, for they are also in a quest for both a history and a legitimacy beyond the one provided by popularity and widespread use and acceptability. One of the more striking aspects of digital culture lies in its almost continuous, uninterrupted dimension (we ought to say almost hourly, for most users): it permeates (if not characterizes) a new daily life marked by new agencies that manage our presence, our communication, and our perception and representation of ourselves and of others. Thus, a new geography is mapped out by the digital environment, one that takes into account the "real geography" (cybertography),[2] but also one that transforms it into the site of a new life from role-playing games to Second Life.[3] Along with this new geography of the digital environment, we witness a growing concern for what I would call authenticity in the virtual. This chapter is an effort to capture some of the elements of this authenticity and its potential implications for forms of political organization and participation. Virtual authenticity is not to be explained by a transfer of a well-known and ultimately problematic category from one model to another; it is not to be restricted to a shift from the real to the virtual. Instead, it consists in the elaboration and experimental development of ways of being within the digital environment that are, so to speak, native, relying on digital habits and customs, taking advantage of digital tools and technologies, and reflecting a concern for norms and values that are predominantly those of digital culture. Virtual authenticity is also motivated by an activist desire, by a will to transform and shape the other, the real world that is becoming more dependent on the digital in general.

I. A Tale of Two Cities

Blogging is perhaps one of the greatest success stories of the emerging digital environment. According to David Sifry, the founder of Technorati, his service is tracking a staggering 57 million blogs as of October 2006.[4] Such a large number, even when taking into account the inactive or abandoned blogs, demonstrates the popularity and the penetration of the model across countries, languages, and cultures. This success has also caused traditional media to adapt blogs for some of their services in order not to be left behind by such a movement.[5] Some have even resorted to what are known as "fake" blogs for advertising purposes.[6] Blogging has challenged established journalism and plays an increasingly important role in the political life across national borders (presidential elections in the United States and France, and China and Iran are primary examples of the potential of blogs in "closed societies"). It has also almost instantly created a large body of authors and brought new technologies to a remarkable number of users and thus introduced and normalized new practices in the digital environment.

While many critics question the value and the longevity of blogging, it is evident that it has been the source of significant changes in the relations between digital and nondigital. It has redefined the status of information, of sources and the ways in which individuals as well as groups seek to exchange and evaluate information. Furthermore, and this is the most important factor from our point of view in this chapter, blogging is at the origin of new models and new technologies that are radically reshaping the conventional information production models as much as significant parts of the digital environment. Thus, blogging as an essentially social and intellectual forum of interaction and knowledge production invites us to think about its structure and the ways in which it puts into place forms of membership and modalities of participation and group organization. In order to think through the self-structuring of blogs, I choose the model of the city as a foundation of the political, and, for starters at least, an essay by Émile Benveniste that discusses the differences between the Greek and the Roman models of the city. This chapter, it goes without saying, not only focuses on blogs, but also on "social software" in general from Wikis to all the current desktop and Web tools that are based on some form of collective authorship, sharing, and creation.

The essay was initially published in 1970 under the title "Deux modèles linguistique de la cité."[7] Its argument is seemingly simple and exploits an opposition between Latin and Greek, that is to say between the couple *civis/civitas* and *polís/politès*.

The Latin *civitas* is an abstract in the form—*tàs* derived from *civis*. But what is the meaning of *civis?* Benveniste shows, through a lengthy and erudite discussion, that the accepted translation of *civis* as *citizen* is false or at least inaccurate. According to him, "one is *civis* of an other *civis* before being *civis* of a specific city." In other words, the Latin signifies first and foremost a relationship of reciprocity and interdependence between two individuals or two groups. Thus, the *civitas* is none other than the set of *civis*. And *civis* designates a social status of reciprocity instead of indicating a membership in an abstract and determining entity like a city. It is no surprise to find that for Benveniste the accurate translation of *civis* is "concitoyen" or "fellow citizen."

The classical Greek model of citizenship could not be more different from the Latin one. In Greek, *Polís* defines both the citizens *(politès)* and their citizenship. It specifies the rules of membership (origin, place of birth, etc.), the rights of participation in the activity of the city as well as the ensuing responsibilities and privileges associated with citizenship. More importantly, it marks a separation between those who belong to the city and those who are outside of its geographical and legal boundaries. It is striking that in most European languages the Greek model of citizenship has been the dominant one (a choice laden with irony since Greece is celebrated as the birthplace of democracy: the model founded on exclusivity of membership grounds, at least in popular mythology, modern forms of democracy). It goes without saying that such a linguistic conception has its political and cultural consequences.

So, if we accept this simplified conceptual opposition between the Greek and the Latin models, where does the blogosphere fit into this picture? Is it more like a Greek city or does it resemble, in its flexibility and reliance on complex forms of reciprocity and exchange, the Latin *civis?*

The network is a decentralized environment; it does not recognize nor does it have a single authority nor does it work according to a unique model. The digital environment has grown and evolved in large part in response to this decentralization, which has worked against efforts to manage its organization. The absence of an overdetermined center (despite the natural aggregation and formation of diverse, interconnected clusters) puts into relief the fluid and reciprocal relations at the core of blogging. While authorities form rather rapidly and tend to concentrate around a relatively small number of nodes, it remains true that users can easily shift and modify their position within the blogosphere. This flexibility is characteristic of the digital presence.

But what is perhaps most interesting at this stage about Benveniste's observations is that they invite us to interrogate the spatial metaphors that are used to designate blogging activity, especially in terms of structure, organization, and modalities of memberships and recognition. The emergence of blogging clusters is slowly shaping traffic but, perhaps more importantly, it is determining the relevant issues significant to the underlying technology and its formal development and deployment. Blogspace, in this instance, is a flexible public sphere where gatherings are constituted by intersecting domains, each defined by a set of commonly shared interests and an ever- growing number of pointers and links. The spread of news from one domain to another resembles to a large degree the structure of rumor and the ways in which it can either create a new reality or modify the perception of an event. Underlying such discursive activity are forms of mutual recognition and relay, forms that actualize the virtual assembly of a community in the open-ended space of the blog city. Benveniste's Roman model is enlightening here because it puts into relief the interdependence of the technological and the discursive in the constitution and formation of the production, distribution and reception of both identities and knowledge. A brief look at the rapid development and transformation of aggregators, blog-related protocols and norms, the adoption of neighborhood and related concepts as an important metaphor, points to the epistemological underpinnings of this new and problematic production of

knowledge (in various forms and formats) and their reflection of the map
of the territory of the blogosphere. In other words, the spatial characteristics of the network shape the concentration of authoritative or knowledge centers and their interrelations. For example, how do tags and their
growing adoption via various folksonomies reshape our hierarchical evaluation and organization of knowledge, and how will they influence the
current model of search engines and the role they play in directing traffic
toward sources of information?[8] What are the new forms of authority
emerging from these practices and how do they interact with currently established ones (this applies to journalism as well as to politics and at times
to some scientific research and publication)?

It would seem that a new social contract, informed by the new realities
of the digital environment and its evolving literacy, is under development,
one that will be well suited to fully accept the challenges posed to copyright, authorship, and intellectual property, not to mention economic models. Furthermore, how will these new knowledge-production conditions
affect the academy (publishing, peer review, and Open Access), historical
discourse, and the political sphere? These questions go well beyond blogging and blogs, but they point to their unmistakable impact on the nature
of information in the digital environment and especially on the role they
play and will continue to play in orienting technological developments with
immediate and lasting cultural, social, and political implications.

But perhaps one of the more interesting dimensions of blogs is the
underlying conception of community they put into place and the ways in
which they challenge current models and their political and social manifestations. Along with the emerging community model instituted by the
popular use of blogs and their extensions, we also have the shift away from
the hierarchical organization and presentation of information to a more
semantic and "ontological" model, founded on the proliferation of categories and tags, whether user generated or centrally organized. Despite all
the difficulties with tags, it is clear nonetheless that they have opened up
the way for a more flexible and adaptable form for marking published
material and for marking authorship. A tag, as an independent form
of reading, associates a contextual interpretation or appreciation of an
item (normally a file) with a reader who is also an author. A tag modifies
not only the relations between the original authorship and the material

authored; it also introduces a difference that is digital: it shifts, or at least can shift, the meaning and the significance of a digital object and its status within the meaning-producing hierarchy from its content to an associated description that is exterior.[9] While tags may suffer, in some ways, from the narrowness if not the impoverishment of what we might call "keyword" culture, they can nevertheless, if properly used, open up public space for a new methodology for valorizing information and its transformation into new knowledge. In the end, tags, a product of blogging culture, display the flexibility of the communitarian model behind the tools and the intricate dependencies on authorship models and their variations within the evolving digital environment. They introduce, in a manner of speaking, a second order of authorship, one that, while not modifying the original content or its attribution, displaces it nonetheless into a space in which it is associated with another form of authorship. This can be applied to any object, to any item that can be accessed via the digital environment. For an interesting case, we can point to a service that encourages its users to associate photos and tags with dictionary words and to measure their popularity and their "affective" status or value.[10] Thus, even language and its words can be subjected to the tagging dimension of digital literacy, promising a potential modification of usage within the limits of a virtual community. One is even tempted to think of this expansion of digital literacy in terms similar to the opposition, in seventeenth-century France, between the Court and the City in the establishment of acceptable usage. In this instance, we would have not only a rivalry between digital and offline, but also, within the digital itself, between conflicting appreciations of literacy.

Benveniste's two cities have allowed us to frame a discussion of blogs in terms that are essentially focused on community, order, and organization. But we will need to complement it with other models of the city, especially the Greek *polis*, in order to grasp fully its value for an appreciation of the emerging digital environment. While these observations are of a somewhat abstract nature, we shall shortly return to them in detail in order to elaborate some of the implications of the practices they are making possible for both the digital environment and the political sphere. But first, a brief survey of what blogs are and how they are produced.

II. Blogs: A Brief Introduction

It has become difficult to talk of blogs, as they have succeeded in becoming commonplace remarkably rapidly, owing in part to press coverage of bloggers and of their impact, especially on political issues, but also because of the growth of easy-to-use tools that allow for the quick creation and publishing of individual blogs.[11] But perhaps it is nevertheless useful to start with the simplest questions: What is a blog and what are some of its basic components? A blog is generally a publishing outlet, organized in reverse chronological order and frequently authored by a single individual (although we are seeing an increasing trend toward collective blogs). A blog does not have to focus on a specific topic or subject matter and can cover a set of wide-ranging issues. What distinguishes it are the structural elements of the post and the accompanying components of the blog. A post is normally brief (few paragraphs, although you may have lengthy entries), that is, either a commentary on a recent story or a reporting of a story. The post frequently includes links to sources of the story in question as well as to other commentaries and analysis. And each post, in principle, should also have a Permalink or a link to the permanent location of the entry, a TrackBack link (or a link that can be used by other blogs and automated discovery systems to alert bloggers as to who else has either linked to the post or written an entry of their own related to it). TrackBacks are useful when trying to examine the ecosystem of a blog and to measure the spread of a particular story or entry, that is to say, when one is either trying to generate analytics concerning blogs that are either similar or to see how popular a particular entry is and how many transformations and citations it has received. TrackBack has, however, fallen victim to spammers (spammers flooded blogs and hosts with fake or unrelated TrackBacks) and is currently broken.[12] Blog entries also tend to indicate the day and time of the original publication as well as the author's handle or name. In brief, a blog is a personal publishing platform that, even in its simplest implementation, can allow broad exposure and immediate publicity. It is also a format that mimics the structure of the journal, highlighting the temporal dimension of writing and the interaction with other sources of information.

Blogs also have sidebars, or a column (some blogs now come in three columns in order to accommodate the need for more "permanent" information and ads) that normally contains a section about the author of the blog (frequently called a Profile and on some a Colophon where you can read about the author, the tools used to create and design the blog), a link to the archives of the blog (and the archives can be organized by chronological order, i.e., month and year, by tag or category, etc.), a Calendar that highlights days of publication of entries, a Blogroll or a set of links to other blogs read by the creator of the blog (and Blogrolls have become rather sophisticated where you can specify your relation to each of the links), a list of recent entries and recent comments, and finally, a link or links to syndication feeds to the blog. Syndication feeds are links to an RSS or Atom aggregation version of the blog that make it possible for readers to subscribe to your blog. In this fashion, their online or desktop Aggregator downloads every new entry published on your blog. You may choose, as the author of the blog, what kind of feed to generate, that is, whether to give your subscribers access to excerpts of entries or whether to publish full entries, among other details. Syndication is increasingly important because of its integration into most desktop tools (from e-mail clients to stand-alone Aggregators to browsers) and because it fundamentally changes the relations between author, publisher, and reader. With an Aggregator, a reader does not have to visit a blog. And, furthermore, readers can choose to have the subscription feeds appear on their systems in a manner of their choosing by applying simple CSS style sheets. In other words, an Aggregator separates content from form and highlights the value of what has been called micro-information engendered by the structure of blog posts. Furthermore, Aggregators record and display all changes to an entry, allowing immediate access to the editorial work of the author and the successive layers of modification that go into composing a post. This feature is obviously complex and can lead to some critical analysis of finished or polished products, especially in the case of "sensitive" material. At any rate, it is clear that "authorship" is both "strengthened" and "weakened" by aggregation and, if anything, it is in the process of being radically redefined. Aggregation feeds can also support enclosures where authors can include multimedia files (audio for podcasts or video for VBlogging [or VideoBlogging], or even sponsored ads). Even with this brief presentation of blogs, we can see why they have successfully become the new "home pages" on the Web, almost completely eliminating the by now "old-fashioned" static sites and home pages. They have become one of the more visible new symbols of one's digital presence. Because of their flexibility and their widespread availability, they are behind what we call "citizen journalism" and "participatory publishing." But we shall return to these broader philosophical issues later.

Blogs also can have a banner that is commonly an image chosen by the author. Banners can include active hyperlinks to other sites or fixed local ages where the author makes available different material. One of the more popular features of current blogs is the inclusion of publicly shared material that is stored on sites like Flickr (where you can upload photographs for free). In this fashion, the blog has become the new and ever-changing version of the distributed desktop from which the user can write and publish text, pictures, audio and video, and share links and references as well as files stored online. This model has now become more important with the rise of Mashups and services like Yahoo!'s Pipes.

You can author blogs either from online services or via blogging tools that work from the desktop or from a browser. Blogger, for instance, now offers the possibility of posting directly from Microsoft Word (on Windows). Often, you have a search capacity integrated into the sidebar, allowing your readers to search the content of your blog.

There are basically two kinds of blogs: one that is managed by the user directly from her server and one that is hosted by a third party. Hosted solutions are perhaps currently the most popular and there exists a large choice of options, although perhaps the best known are Blogger (now owned by Google), Microsoft's Spaces, and WordPress, to name only a few. Among the for-pay hosting providers there is TypePad (from the creators of MovableType,[13] and now the owners of LiveJournal and of Vox as well). Both services offer easy setup, a selection of templates and designs, and WYSIWYG (What You See Is What You Get) HTML editors for the blogs.[14] Furthermore, some of them provide easy setup for categories, tags, photo albums, and calendars, whereas in the case of some of the free services, setting up such tools requires a bit more effort. Obviously, there are other services as well.

For the server setup, there are many blogging tools currently available, but perhaps the two most popular ones are MovableType and WordPress. They are powerful and can accommodate large corporate blogs as well as individual ones. They also allow for the creation of multiple blogs on the same domain and for multiple authors on a single blog. Furthermore, they can be tied to a domain or reside in a subdirectory. For setting them up, the user needs to have access to a server and be able to upload and modify file permissions. The user must be able to have a database (most commonly, either a MySQL or Postgres). Once all files are installed, you can manage and configure all other aspects of the blog from a Web interface. Both tools allow for the configuration and generation of RSS and Atom feeds. You can also choose to ping (or to inform sites that collect such information) servers every time you post a new entry.

One of the main difficulties with blogs is the rise in Comments and TrackBack spams. Automated bots try to write a large number of Comments with links to gambling or pornographic sites. They do the same for TrackBacks. There are currently a number of solutions devised to counter this growing problem: they either require user registration and authentication prior to posting Comments and TrackBacks, or they require some form of third-party authentication of users (such as TypeKey) before allowing users to write comments. There are also tools that blacklist hosts and domain names or keywords that are known to generate spams as well. Finally, a user can post to a blog from a mobile phone, thus leading to the practice of moblogging.

This brief summary of the basic features of blogs is only meant as a background for a discussion of the issues currently raised by the widespread adoption of blogs in a diversity of cultural and political contexts, but before proceeding, a few supplementary remarks.

The popularity of blogging is also interesting because it is the first instance of the success of the Open Source model on a large scale. Most users are not aware of the fact that they are frequently using Open Source tools developed and distributed under the GPL and that the blog designs or the CSS files used to modify the look and feel of blogs are also distributed under the GPL or a similar Open Source license. But beyond this penetration of the Open Source model into the popular use, blogs have created a number of phenomena, from the development of Open Source information resources to the diversification of news sources and the increasing challenge to the "professionalization" of journalism. Citizen journalists now share information, contest the accuracy or the authority of established sources, and are frequently absorbed into the mainstream. Furthermore, press agencies and news organizations are under pressure to compete with the online independent journalists and sources. Some social- networking sites such as Flickr have become the sites of breaking news, often beating conventional media in reporting a story. Obviously, there is a debate about the value of citizen journalism that is ongoing and that tends to concentrate on the value of established journalistic practices and editorial policies and the dangers of free-form publishing. The arguments also invite us to take a closer look at the viability of the new paradigm of deliberative democracy online, its modalities and pitfalls.[15]

Another important aspect of blogs, less visible in the United States and in Europe, is their growing political use against oppressive regimes and the ensuing censorship. Here, we find a more immediately pro-active use of the publishing tools and an exploitation of the flexibility of online publishing and the freedoms it provides. Iran is perhaps the most important and interesting example where we find a mature and complex use of blogs to contest political authority and some of its abusive, authoritarian tendencies. But we can also look to China and some of the Arab countries (especially Saudi Arabia) as well. This political dimension of blogging has led to the development of servers (sometimes supported by Western governments) that allow for anonymous blogging, thus, in theory, protecting the identity of bloggers. We shall not examine in great detail the rise in censorship and the technologies it uses as well as its cultural and political components. One last remark on this topic suffices for the moment: blogging has also led to an increase in filtering and censorship in countries where established political authority is often criticized and contested. And obviously, as in the United States and Europe, we now have a generation of politicians who are bloggers as well. This will eventually lead, in my opinion, to a shift in the modes of public debates and to important changes in the "handling" of political messages.

III. Public Spaces and Virtual Autochthony

Now that we have briefly surveyed blogs and their infrastructure, we can revisit the linguistic model of the two cities proposed by Benveniste in order to see if it provides us with any insight into an understanding of the potential of blogs and related technologies in shaping frameworks for communities. Benveniste's essay, to limit ourselves to a simple point here, highlights the importance of grammatical relations and their association with a place, with a territory, or, better yet, with an identity intimately associated with a marked space. Thus, in the Greek model, the *polís* is the defining term and entity: citizenship is a function of a set of variables related to its structure from genealogy to territory. The Roman model, on the other hand, proceeds in the opposite way: the association of individuals and their mutual relations define and determine the *civitas*. The Roman model is first and foremost relational: it is based on forms of reciprocity, recognition, and ultimately solidarity among individuals. It is a society formed by qualities that are as Benveniste says "distinctive" of each citizen. The importance of this opposition between the two models lies in the relations between citizenship and space, or, to put it in other terms, it derives from the ways in which it identifies belonging and legitimacy to a connection that is marked by spatial relations and their social and political symbolizations. Everyone can become a Roman citizen, whereas only those born in Athens can claim to be Athenians. On the one hand, a form of autochthony, on the other, a relatively open model of citizenship.

Even with this rapid summary of the opposition between Greek and Roman, we can see the relevance to the current digital environment and its associated framework for a digital identity. While language remains a marker of identity in the digital world, it is less of an absolute symbol. The import of technologies such as blogs and Wikis, as well as the growing number of social- networking sites, lies precisely in the continuous creation of modular communities with relatively open memberships and identities that are tied to a shared interest and not to fixed forms. The fluidity and the rapid changes that characterize such communities, which appear to some as merely fads or passing fashions, are also characteristic of a flexible and experimental form of virtual citizenship that is being slowly but surely developed. This experimental construction of community building relies rather heavily on the technology and is often driven not by an ideological or a social choice but instead by unforeseen uses of technological platforms. In other words, the technology is making possible practices that are essentially social but within the digital environment, and that require a dose of digital literacy that will, in the end, have social and political

consequences. We are perhaps to think of membership in some online
communities as a form of education that, like any such pedagogical experience, can shape and form both individuals and groups. If the current
digital environment is more akin to Benveniste's Roman model, it is creating a multiplicity and a diversity of Romes, a set of digital spaces where
membership is defined by a variety of factors and that can share intersecting membership. Furthermore, and this is part of the evolution of the current technology in its social dimension, we are witnessing a convergence
of such sites thanks to publicly available and open tools. Thus, it is relatively easy to share photos from a Flickr account on an individual blog, or,
perhaps more interestingly, it is equally easy to share one's readings (via
RSS feeds) with visitors to one's blog. Such relatively simple applications of
social aspects of technology are significant because they create communities
based on multiple values and multiple interests. They also create new spheres
of influence and, ultimately, new public spheres that go beyond national
borders and linguistic or cultural determinations.

In fact, to return to our Greek *polís* for a moment, the current digital
environment shares some significant similarities with the Greek city, despite the affinity with the Roman model and the loss of autochthony implied by digital identity and its insertion within the digital environment.
It is not my intention here to establish a simple resemblance and a linear
similarity between the current practices emerging within digital culture
and the Greek city, especially when considered as the original model for
our Western democratic model and the foundation for the conduct and
management of public affairs. Instead, in choosing to look at some of the
details of the often-celebrated Greek miracle and its Roman counter-
part, my objective is to highlight the spatial (and, in our case here, I would
add the virtual) dimension of the model and the temporality it activates.
In both instances we have a potential for participation that is linked to a
form of recognized presence and its symbolisms and manifestations.
Spatiality is essential because it not only designates the site of the political, but it also organizes and orders its accepted practices and norms.
Such a function has, it goes without saying, an important role to play in
the valorization of emerging institutional practices: What is acceptable
and what is not? What is valued, what is exchangeable, and what is possible? If the Greek city is a site of autochthony, the digital equivalent is

its dissolution.[16] It signals the shift to a new public sphere and an emerging social space.

Elaborating on Jean-Pierre Vernant's observations, Pierre Vidal-Naquet reminds us that the Greek *polís* creates a new space, a new social space that is endowed with a particular identity: "The city creates an altogether new social space centered on the *agora* with its 'foyer commun' where general problems are debated, a space in which power no longer resides in a palace but in the center, *es méson*. It is in the center that the orator who speaks for the general good stands. To this space corresponds a civic time."[17] The city is first and foremost a spatial displacement, from the court to the center of the city, a center chosen and defined by the citizens, by their collective discussion and will. While the center remains essential as a symbol of equality, it requires a limited and defined space. If the ancient Greek city and its democratic practices are distinguished by a move from the palace to the city center, what is the digital equivalent of such a displacement and how are we to recognize it in the current situation of technological evolution? The digital city, or perhaps we should say cities, are by definition decentralized, with their own spatial characteristics, and yet they all have a home. This home has also a Greek precedent or equivalent (in Vidal-Naquet's description, it is the "foyer commun"), and its goddess as well.[18]

The Greek city as a model allows us to capture the spatial significance of the digital environment, especially in its current "social" phase, and to appreciate some of its practices and their cultural symbolism. For instance, each social- networking hub has a number of characteristics that include some or all of the following:

(a) A common entry point that is either a site or an integrated version into a browser or a desktop application. Normally, these entry points have the same look and feel and try to recreate a familiar and distinctive environment.

(b) Access is controlled according to hierarchy of privileges and rights (who is admitted, who can read, who can comment, who can post and who can tag and share, etc.).

(c) A set of rules that govern the community: these mostly relate to some forms of controls over speech and intellectual property.

(d) A set of tools that allow each user to manage his presence and his privacy within the community.

(e) A form of governance of the community that each user must agree to before being admitted.

These brief features highlight the city-like features of each community. They provide a combination of rational and reasonable rules for membership while taking advantage of technological potential. From our perspective here, they are virtual public spaces with their own *agoras*, with their own cultures, and ultimately their own politics. Their significance stems in part from the fact that they are becoming public spheres that frequently replace the public sphere; they are becoming digital sites for discussing and perhaps deciding on questions of common interest. In short, they are operating a displacement from the public sphere as we have known it into a fluid and intersecting set of public spheres. What characterizes these emerging public spheres is first the fact that they are fundamentally digital in nature: they are at once distributed, and able to integrate technological practices and digital literacy with their potential for social and political activism. They rely on the polyphonic nature of digital identity and they translate social networking into socio-technological practices. Thus the creation of multiple and often intersecting communities depends not only on shared interests but also on equally shared or open technologies. It is not my intention here to discuss the benefits of such a model and set of practices nor to evaluate their political role, but simply to point out that they are political in a manner that is historical and thus subject to an eventually comparative approach to the study of the digital environment and the emerging digital literacy. The convergence of social, if not virtual socializing, practices (and here we recall our brief discussion of technology as a potential civilizing process) and digital technology, while at times alienating, can also operate a displacement from passive to active or at least participatory membership. Simple activities like tagging or commenting can become initiatory performances, slowly enticing users into becoming more involved and more adventurous in their digital wanderings. These activities also create micro-communities that can evolve into more significant groupings based on specific and at times narrow affinities. The key factor remains that the technology is both virtually socializing and at times socially alienating. But the technology is determining because it shapes to a large degree what is and what is not possible and decides what is and what is not accessible. Furthermore, its culture shapes what is known and how it can be known (access as a form of knowledge is one of the main features of the digital environment).

It is tempting to describe the digital environment as the site of emerging democratic practices on a global scale, opening up access and broadening participation to those who had been denied such participation in the past. It certainly is true that the digital has become, in some instances, the site of effective contestation of political authority and has generated a culture of political resistance embedded within the digital environment and its digital literacy. Thus, we can point to examples of blogs or similar sites that give voice to those who have rarely had such an opportunity in the past, making it possible to create a viable forum for political and social action.[19] In these cases, the concept of digital literacy needs to be expanded further, for it covers not only the ability to interact and participate within the digital environment. But it also implies a broader cultural and political literacy, one that takes advantage of the technology in order to make available and accessible ideas and opinions hitherto either altogether ignored or limited to the specialist. Digital activism demonstrates the political potency of the technology and the practices it makes possible, but it also points to the need to reflect on the relations between digital literacy and the political. In the same manner that literacy radically transformed the political sphere, digital literacy has the potential to reinvent political culture. By the same token that reading became an essential feature of citizenship, digital literacy, because of its hybrid nature (combining the mastery of technology with the management of governance and rules for participating in a multiplicity of communities), promises to produce a new social bond that is inherently digital, with its own rules and norms.

Since we have been discussing the digital environment in terms derived from classical models, it is useful to provide an example that would illustrate the digital adaptation of such paradigms. The classical city is in large part organized in such a way as to manage violence and values (economic as much as ethical and political). The digital city has its own violence, an extension of "traditional" violence, but with a technological twist. At its simplest, it is represented by what has been termed cyberbullying. Cyberbullying is revealing because it affects mostly (but not exclusively) younger users across cultures and nations and because it has led to the drafting of laws to curb its spread.[20] Wikipedia defines cyberbullying as follows: "online bullying is the term used to refer to bullying and harassment by use of electronic devices though means of e-mail, instant messaging, text messages, blogs, mobile phones, pagers, and websites."[21] Cyberbullying is perhaps the first widespread form of digital violence: it is first and foremost digital (although it consists of the extension and adaptation of well-known forms of verbal violence); it exploits the openness of the digital environment and the polyphony of digital identity by circulating abusive information or making available private and confidential information; it converts and subverts digital presence and the virtual digital sphere into a space of violence. The more a society is connected the more it is subject to this and other forms of digital violence. A classic example is South Korea, perhaps one of the most connected countries in the world today. According to a story on online violence in the BBC: "In a society where social networking is as popular as meeting up for a drink, information spreads quickly. Online mobs first demonise those they disagree with, then the victim's home address, credit card details, and even their boss's phone numbers get passed around. All of Korea's police stations now have a cyber-terror unit to help deal with the problem."[22] The emergence of digital violence, beyond the theft of digital identity, invites us to evaluate the model of digital communities and the technological framework underlying their organization in terms of questions that are familiar from our classical models: how to manage violence within the emerging public sphere, and how to negotiate between the freedoms offered by the changes in citizenship while protecting the privacy of individual citizens; how to formulate effective strategies to face the emerging digital threats without necessarily curtailing or reducing the freedoms it makes possible; how to determine the social rules and models of governance to adopt in the new digital environment, especially when considering social interactions and their dynamics. The classical city is perhaps more relevant than one would think, for it succeeded in formalizing the divide between violence and public spaces: on the one hand, the center, the most public of all spaces and the most visible symbol of the new social and political reality; on the other, a more intimate and familial space, the more restricted space where membership is more strongly determined. By analogy, we can say that the virtual public sphere resembles the city whereas the private virtual sphere or the need for a protected digital privacy echoes the balance introduced into the representation of the city by Hestia and her household.

While cyberbullying is only one concentrated form of digital violence, we can see a slew of variations within the digital environment. Privacy, and particularly digital privacy, is becoming in more urgent need of not only protection but, I would argue, understanding. In other words, a key dimension of digital literacy consists in comprehending the complexity of privacy in the digital environment, for digital violence is always a form of abuse of digital privacy. But digital privacy remains an elusive and con- tested concept.[23] Digital privacy requires a new acceptance of private space and of its relations with the emerging virtual public spheres. It requires a negotiated settlement between government's tendency to regulate and, in the digital age, to collect, store, and share information about citizens, and the citizens' rights to equal access to the information and its use.

IV. Return of the Voice?

Our classical models of the city led us to an examination of some essential aspects of the emerging digital environment and its social dimensions. The technologies at work in the environment have modified not only the status and locus of the public sphere, but they have also revived or brought back some other, more traditional variables. A case in point is the voice and its reemergence into the digital environment thanks to the growing pop- ularity of podcasting. While podcasting derives its name from a gadget (Apple's iPod), it in effect describes the activity of creating and publishing online a multimedia recording that is made available to users via either an RSS feed or other sites. In short, a podcast is an online published record- ing that is accessible via RSS (but not exclusively). What is so unique about podcasting and how might we account for its remarkable success and popularity? And what does it say about the role and status of voice in the digital environment?

While podcasting is deceptively simple, it is important to keep in mind its flexibility. It allows users to listen to their chosen podcasts on a variety of instruments: computers, iPods, mobile phones, portable media players, in their cars, and so on. In other words, it first extends the penetration of the virtual digital sphere into new zones. It also, obviously, extends existing and well-established communication technologies, most notably radio. Podcasting can also be seen as democratizing a communication medium that so far has been limited to either governments or rich corporations, thus allowing any user with a computer, a microphone, and a server or access to a public server to participate in previously inaccessible media. In this case, we can say that podcasting continues the movement of digital literacy in opening up all forms of authorship to its participants, reducing the differences between authors and readers, and here between radio broadcasters and listeners.[24] Podcasting represents a clear instance of the revolutionary potential of digital technologies because it demonstrates, perhaps more than any other currently available set of tools, the potential for shifting the hierarchy that has dominated the relations between information producers and information consumers. But it also illustrates how social practices emerge from a convergence of tools and adaptation of known technologies. It destabilizes further the "traditional" media by providing a sophisticated outlet for amateur productions that can now rival the most polished corporate productions.

But podcasting offers also a new marker of digital identity: the voice. In this instance, the voice becomes an added value identifier, one that creates a familiarity and that, at least within the digital environment, much as in "real" life, goes beyond its biometric elements. The voice can become the site of recognition, a recognition not based on biometric samples but grounded instead in the interaction between podcaster and listener. This interaction, however, is no longer limited to a public zone, but has moved instead into the more private corners of the digital environment. Much like the instruments and technologies it relies on, it transfers a form of privacy into the open and public space. It reintroduces a form of distinctive individualism into the otherwise all-too-visible digital environment. Such individualism also transforms its instruments into markers of exclusion; an individual with his iPod and his earpiece is actively separating himself from the crowd; he is consciously staying out of the public space. Listening to a podcast in public is an antisocial gesture but also a manifestation of digital individuality within the traditional environment. If indeed it is true that hell is the music of others, then podcasting is the digital private paradise. It creates an intimate space that imports the digital into any environment. And it is, first and foremost, a listening exercise. Silent, it makes room anew for a form of reading that had almost disappeared, reading aloud. And it therefore brings back to the center of the digital environment the role of the orator (invoked by Vidal-Naquet in his description of the new space created by the Greek *polis*) and of oratory arts, of the rhetoric of reading and delivery, of the modulation of voice and pathos, of the powers of persuasion and of rhetorical ethos. However, we are no longer in the city center where all the citizens come to assemble; instead, we are perhaps in public, but in actuality, in a privacy made possible by the digital tools.

If I am emphasizing the private dimension of podcasting it is in order to highlight their passive features, but this passivity is not only restricted to the act of listening; it is also integral to the tools and technologies employed. iPods and similar media players allow users to download content. The software designed to manage podcasting and similar digital media productions are also modeled on a passive paradigm; creators or podcasters upload and make available their productions and users can subscribe and download them. So far, podcasting has been, in this particular case, uniquely old media. Some of the reasons for this are obvious and they mostly stem from the history of media players and their support for Digital Rights Management, thus enforcing a one-way relation between content and its distribution. But there is no technological reason for not allowing podcasting tools and software to become interactive.[25] To use Dave Winer's terms, the podcast player must become a platform and it should be "Read-write, two-way, should be able to record and connect with a publishing system for automatic upload and feed production. Must be a platform, that is, people other than the manufacturer can add apps."[26] The limitations of the current podcasting framework reflect the hybrid or transitional phase of the technology and its negotiation between offering users access and satisfying copyright holders with sufficient protections. The net result, however, is a diminished experience within the digital environment and impoverishment of users' experience in general.

If, as I have argued, podcasting signals a digital return of the voice and its rhetorical density, the technology must support its full deployment: it has to move beyond the current model of subscribe and deliver into a more dynamic and creative one that will be subscribe, publish, and deliver. For the implications of such a change are similar to the ones we observe in other digital destabilizations of inherited authorship models and their social and legal frameworks. With increased connectivity and flexibility of media players to become media authorship platforms, the nature of the virtual public sphere is likely to change, as will its forms of organization and structuring principles. It will certainly become richer and more diverse, but it will also allow for the revival of cultural forms and even of languages in danger of extinction. For despite the normative, collective pressure, podcasting and similar digital activities are inherently receptive to individual and marginal, if not minority, expressions and points of view. It is in this specific manner that digital literacy exploits its version of the public sphere in order to make room for cultural forms of identity. Much like the individualism of listening to podcasts within the public space, the tools of podcasting, if extended, can also accommodate a multiplicity of cultural identities and traditions within the digital environment. The political model, again decentralized and distributed, allowing multiple forms of memberships and participation, is primarily social. The digital city is a virtual city inhabited not only by images and texts, but by increasingly welcoming voices in the fullest sense of the word.

V. Searching for a New Home: Web OS, or Digital Migration

Podcasting as a platform is but one aspect of the evolution of the digital environment into an increasingly complex site for authoring and creating, and not only for surfing and reading. This evolution is most visible today in what we can call Web OS, and it is best illustrated by Google and the manner in which it has assembled all of its services in order to offer its users a network operating system and framework that can replace the desktop operating system and its applications. While network operating systems have been around for a long time and efforts to introduce dumb terminals or "empty" network stations that act as merely access points have come and gone, the current trend appears to be taking hold and succeeding in attracting an increasing number of users. The shift from the centrality of the desktop into a Web OS accompanies the current trends in the digital environment and the growth of the need of continuous access to not only information but to one's own information. For a culture that values uninterrupted access and connection, a Web OS would appear ideal. But this shift mirrors also some of the spatial displacements we have already discussed in the location of the virtual public sphere, its nature and its structure.

But why has a network OS failed whereas a Web OS appears to be succeeding? The answer, at least in part, resides in the difference between a network and the Web. A network, when discussing a network OS, means a controlled network, one owned by a company, an institution, or a government, and one that requires, in some cases, a dedicated machine in order to access it. A Web OS, on the other hand, is one that is owned by a company (Google, Yahoo!, Microsoft, etc.) but that is accessible from everywhere there is a point of access and a browser. Furthermore, it is no coincidence that the current players in the field of Web OS are predominantly search engines, for there exists an intimate association between the cultural status and evolution of searching and the history of Web OS. Web OS basically describes a set of Web services and applications that can make it possible for a user not to own a computer. Thus, a user can have his e-mail via Google Mail, his documents and spreadsheets on Docs, his Google Calendar, his images on Picasa, and his own blog, RSS feeds, and home page. In other words, Web OS offers the equivalent of a desktop with the added benefit of a Web presence, except, of course, for the local archive.[27] The initial version of these integrated offers had one outstanding limitation (besides the archiving): the absence of an individual Web identity for the user, an identity that is tied to a personal domain. That is no longer a problem with the latest offer from Google: individuals can tie their services to their own domain if they have control over its DNS. But beyond this expansion, why is it that search engines and not makers of operating systems dominate this model? Operating systems are trying to integrate search into their model, allowing users to search both locally stored material and online sources, in the same way that search engines are bringing their expertise to the desktop by offering users tools to perform similar queries. Such offerings come with their own risks, increasing users' exposure to new vulnerabilities, but for our purposes here, the crucial element remains the assembly of Web features and components that are an equivalent (and at times even more) of a desktop system.

The displacement toward such a Web presence constitutes a crucial step in the evolving digital literacy because it inaugurates a new attitude toward data and information. Desktop systems are privately owned; they are under the control of users; they can be connected or disconnected; and users have the freedom to create and delete information at will. In a Web OS, while the data are nominally owned by its creator, its archive is owned and controlled by the provider. Acceptance of Web OS amounts to a cultural change in the nature of information ownership and the values we attach to it. It represents the digital form of a cultural migration or, to put it differently, it represents a migration toward a fully digital environment. In this fashion, it stands for a shift toward new homes, new digital homes with new identities and new rights, privileges, obligations, and responsibilities. The new environment, while familiar and in a sense comforting (continued access to one's own information from almost everywhere), is also radically different from previous models for its implementation of a participatory culture. In this case, the digital city is moving in new directions that call for closer inspection and evaluation, if only to think through its implications for the nature and materiality of digital identity and its support.

While search engines, in their earliest incarnations, were exactly what their names say—tools that allowed users to search indexed material—they quickly modified the nature of what is stored and how it is presented. Early on, the size of the Index was essential, along with relevance and accuracy (and these remain so today), but owing to the practices generated by the success of Google in particular, a slew of fads sprang up. Thus we had Google Juice (presence and rank of an individual in the Google Index), Googlism (what Google knows or thinks it knows about an individual), and similar fashions. Such fads are indicative of the forms of presence generated by search engines and their narcissistic association with digital identity. The Index, in this case, is no longer simply the sum, the neutrally evaluated archive, but it is instead the site for a demonstration of individual distinction. With a new civilization comes new values and new forms of social hierarchy and class, and within the digital environment, presence on an Index is but one highly significant form of such a social status. Digital migration thus operates not only by moving the locus of a stable center from the network into the virtual space of digital culture; it also functions by creating and popularizing new forms of presence and appearance, by valorizing new modalities of personal and collective distinction. In short, it works to construct a new digital *polís* with its own rationality, its own territory, its own classes, and ultimately its own barbarians. In the digital city, a barbarian is one who is not present, the individual who has no place, no home, no contact, or simply no connection. A barbarian is indeed the other and the outsider, but one who, either willingly or not, chooses not to participate in the new culture and its civilization. Search engines, while indeed performing a necessary and essential role in facilitating access to information, have also put into place practices that, as they have extended beyond simply the Index and its norms, amount to the foundations of a new order, a digital order firmly grounded in values inspired and formed by technology. It is this expansion of the Index as a valorizing paradigm rooted in a particular cultural heritage (and especially of Google's services and reach) that explains some of the "nationalist" reactions to some of its services. Here, the primary example comes from France and its efforts to oppose Google as alien to European culture.[28] The opposition to the organization of information and the management of its access centers, curiously enough, on its universalist claims and the implications of such claims to specific cultures and their uses of information. In other words, in the reaction against the growth of a search engine index into a provider of culture and of potentially of cultural values, we witness the reemergence of a politics of civilization: on the one hand, an Anglo-Saxon civilization, represented as influenced by a rather simplified utilitarian perspective, and, on the other, a rival universal culture firmly grounded in the traditions of a language and its cultural history. Suffice it to say that while Google may have universalist ambitions, it is not clear that a government-funded search engine (in this case a French one) would be able to incarnate specifically French or European cultural values.[29] The French reaction to Google's ever-expanding role in controlling access to information demonstrates the cultural density of the indexing of information and its association with other digital services. It also showcases the ways in which identities, individual and national and regional, are becoming increasingly subject to what I have called digital migration.

But in another way, Google's Books (an initiative to make available online searchable wholes or parts of books) and Scholar projects illustrate the robustness and power of print culture and its entrenched models. While most public attention has focused on the cultural dimension of the projects and its potential hegemony, it remains the case that such projects are the first realistic proposals for a viable online research environment. In other words (and well beyond the culture wars or the polemic surrounding copyright), these projects constitute an essential component of a digital Web OS in that they provide access to tools and content that transform further the digital environment into an environment for the production and distribution of new knowledge: a digital migration in the direction of a distributed and participatory culture, but one that is so far dominated by one or at the most two entities. Google's eminence in this area stems from the success of its Index and its extension, as a model, into other areas of digital culture. It also speaks to the difficulties of negotiating the intricacies of digital migration, from the politics of cultural identity to the conversion from print to digital.

We started this chapter with a discussion of blogs and cities, and we have come to an examination of digital manifestations of knowledge and its production in the digital environment. Such a trajectory, while not necessarily exemplary, symbolizes the path taken by the civilizing process that is digital culture. New social formations, new values, and new sites for accessing and interacting with them emerge, thanks to digital literacy and its continual negotiation with technology and social practices. If blogs represent the first large-scale step toward easy digital authorship, they are but a transition toward more complex and more sophisticated digital frameworks that are in essence social. The digital environment is fundamentally a digital city with its own rules, its own governance, its own politics and, unfortunately, its own forms of violence. Digital *polis* is neither a utopia nor a promised land: it is a territory that is being invented and shaped by citizens-digiticians.

VI. Wiki Ways

Our initial ventures into digital literacy were based on the changes introduced by technology and the nature of the digital object itself, and the manner in which they lead to new models of reading and authoring. In that context, the Wiki stood out as paradigmatic because it, by design, collapses the differences between readers and authors and provides a continuous archive of all edits and modifications. The unparalleled success of Wikipedia as a source of information has led us to question the credibility of the model, and not only from defenders of traditional sources of expert information. In other words, while Wikipedia's success as a source of information stems from its easy access and its broad linguistic and cultural diversity, its management of information production remains a problem. Its commitment to an open, digital form of authoring that relies on the "wisdom of the crowds"[30] has been called into question. For an example of a variation on the Wikipedia model, we can point to the proposed Citizendium.[31] While Wikipedia is an experiment with rules and governance shaped by the full promise of digital literacy and its values, it still has to address concerns about legitimacy, credibility, and ultimately, responsibility. In this fashion, it stands as the first and most visible structure of the new digital city; an edifice constantly changing, constantly growing and, theoretically at least, constantly improving. It is similar to Google's growing empire and ultimately may prove a competition for its growth and control over access to information sources. But first it has to manage its own version of digital violence, represented by slanderous or inaccurate information about individuals, events, and historical narratives.

Citizendium therefore offers a more controlled format for producing an equivalent to Wikipedia. It proposes to institute a hierarchy of responsibility and expertise into the authoring function of the Wiki in order to avoid the traps of open and anonymous or pseudo-anonymous authorship that plague Wikipedia. And thus, it requires real names from authors, allows for editors who are recognized experts who are authorized to referee content, and creates Constables who will act as the peacemakers of the virtual knowledge city. If I chose to quickly invoke this model, it is not only because of the name of the project and its ties to forms of digital citizenship, but especially in order to point out that digital migration, while successful in some domains, remains currently tied to print models and to their social and scholarly values.[32] The digital city has yet to produce its own, completely digital forms of authority and responsibility other than the current trends and fashions. The recent controversy occasioned by the false claims of some official Wikipedia authors is but a symptom of this quest for a cohesive and coherent paradigm of credibility that is capable of satisfying both the nature and inspiration of the Wiki model and delivering an acceptable and responsible public content. Authorship thus remains, for the time being, an essential category linked to more than a virtual identity because it serves as one of the bases for evaluating content. And, furthermore, debates and polemics about authorship reflect the importance of a perception gap between the status of Wikipedia online and its own understanding of its mission and purpose. Wikipedia's success, both in becoming the dominant reference online as well as its prominence in search indexes, serves only to highlight this difficulty. It is true that Wikipedia, in its description of its own articles, points out the nature of the knowledge it makes available, insisting on the changing nature of its articles and on the need for a recurrent reading in order to fully evaluate the content. Thus:

> As a wiki, articles are never complete. They are continually edited and improved over time, and in general this results in an upward trend of quality, and a growing consensus over a fair and balanced representation of information. Users should be aware that not all articles are of encyclopedic quality from the start. Indeed, many articles start their lives as partisan, and it is after a long process of discussion, debate and argument, that they gradually take on a neutral point of view reached through consensus. Others may for a while become caught up in a heavily unbalanced viewpoint which can take some time— months perhaps—to extricate themselves and regain a better balanced consensus. In part, this is because Wikipedia operates an internal resolution process when editors cannot agree on content and approach, and such issues take time to come to the attention of more experienced editors.[33]

The new form of authorship calls for a different form of reading: entries and articles are to be evaluated over time and only such reading will be able to judge the quality of Wikipedia fairly. The multiple and deliberative authorship calls for an equivalent form of reading, one that is not a rereading in the classical sense of the term, but instead a reading anew each time, but with a particular attention to the archive or to the changes introduced into each text. A Wiki article is thus a fragment or an essay,

constantly open to edits and emendations. Once again we encounter another feature of digital literacy, one that is firmly grounded in a practice
informed and shaped by the nature of the digital object and the specificities of the tools used to create and to manipulate it.

Thus, it is understandable that "Wikipedia is not a place to publish
your own thoughts and analyses or to publish new information not here-
tofore published . . . Wikipedia is not an experiment in democracy or any
other political system. Its primary method of determining consensus is
discussion, not voting. Although editors occasionally use straw polls in an
attempt to test for consensus, polls or surveys may actually impede rather
than assist discussion. They should be used with caution, if at all, and may
not be treated as binding."[34] Therefore, dialogue and discussion over and
against the sheer power of a majority take place within a context where,
over time, accuracy is approached thanks to the anonymous and continuous increase in contributions and the improvement of existing text and entries. Thus we have a space for a guided (and some would argue misguided)
conversation in lieu of a mere majority-driven determination of content: a
deliberative instead of an electoral system, but one that requires some
form of an editorial control that while maintaining anonymity will be
able to ground the increasing demand for accountability and credibility.
Wiki space, therefore, is a discursive space and, like the city, one that is
trying to carve out a specific and unique site for digital persuasion and its
cultural, if not ultimately political, effects. What has been a source of
problems is precisely the lack of visibility and transparency in the setting
and management of this space and its privileged sites, and the encourage-
ment, whether conscious or not, of a mistaken perception of the genesis of
generated content in Wikipedia, especially when controversial or disputed.
And it has to be said that lack of visibility and transparency amount to a
virtual form of reverse censorship. For, for most users, presence or availability on Wikipedia are synonymous with credible, and the phenomenal
popularity of Wikipedia serves only to compound the difficulties.

I certainly do not mean to argue against the promise of the Wikipedia
model or diminish its already impressive achievements. Instead, I mean
simply to point out both the limitations of the current model, particularly
in the current transitional period from print to digital (constrained in
part by the technology itself and the ways in which it problematizes au-

thoring), and the difficulties of managing the new civic space and the
knowledge it is producing without a reflection on the emerging digital
literacy.

But it is also legitimate to ask what Wikipedia is and what it is not, according to its founders and to its current editors, comparing the project
and its early incarnation to its current status as a major source of reference
and information online and to the actual uses now associated with it. The
difference between the theoretical model of managing authorship and
controlling the production and publication of controversial content on the
one hand, and its current symbolic status as the representative of a new,
deliberative, and collective authorship that embodies the promise of free
knowledge of the digital environment on the other, invites a closer examination of the role that literacy, in the strong sense of the term, plays in
shaping both the generation and the reception of information within this
most visible instance of digital culture. How are we to explain, for instance,
the relative failure or unpopularity of WikiBooks and their limitations? Is
it simply because they are much too closely modeled on print books and
thus fail, so to speak, to distinguish themselves; or is it because, owing to
the nature of the book, and especially the scholarly book and its well-
established protocols of annotations and documentation, the book model
represents a step backward for the digital literacy inaugurated by tools
such as Wikipedia? Why is it that articles or entries that are open-ended
by nature and subject to what the Wikipedia project hopes is the natural
tendency toward increased accuracy, credibility, and relevance dominate?
Is this simply a manifestation of the anthological dimension of the learned
digital object as embodied by Wikipedia, or does it instead stand for the
failure of the tools to successfully mirror and capture the book as an object
within the digital environment? Perhaps a quick look at a simple example
will be instructive here.[35]

I chose the William Shakespeare WikiBook because it is in early draft
at this time and because of its potential paradigmatic status,[36] but also
because of the history of the formation of the canonical Shakespearean
corpus and the ways in which it puts into play key concepts we have been
encountering so far. The WikiBook promises (I think naïvely at this point)
to provide its readers with a "reliable text about Shakespeare's works (his
plays and poems). Also, along with every play, there is a brief explanation

of its origins, plot, and themes."[37] In this instance, and at least for the foreseeable future, the WikiBook will not succeed in taking into account the rich scholarship behind the formation of the canonical Shakespeare and especially its relation to the anthological.[38] In this case, and because we are dealing with a literary text, we face a new divide between scholarly or learned disputes and Wiki facts: a divide between print and digital in its early and tentative efforts to produce a reference work on a cultural icon deeply embedded within print culture and its practices. Obviously, it can be argued that WikiBooks are a nascent project and that they will be able to equal if not surpass the printed book if given the time to develop and mature. While this may be true, I am trying to point out here the potential effects of the contradictions of adopting the book as a model for a digital object within an environment that undermines classical forms of authorship and its institutions. Furthermore, unlike scientific discourse, literary discourse is more difficult to normalize and subject to the laws of deliberative consensus. And, curiously enough, such deliberative consensus takes its queue from a fundamentally literary practice that has yet to find its place within the digital environment.

But such a reality is not necessarily an obstacle; instead it calls for new forms of evaluating information and especially for a new aesthetics that requires tolerance. Wiki spaces, much like the blogosphere, are the early incarnations of the emerging digital city. The city, as we know, creates a civic space, but it also creates mechanisms for inclusion and, more importantly, for exclusion, and thus there is the need for new forms of tolerance. The digital city is a new landscape that, as we have seen, by instituting new practices calls for new laws that can accommodate the nature of the digital object and the ways in which it circulates within the digital environment. Access and openness are the vehicles for more than just sharing files and easy communication. They are the emblems for potentially radical social and political changes on a global level, for they legitimate new values. The digital environment is a new form of a city that has yet to finalize its ultimate shape and define its frontiers.

This emerging city echoes in its practices, in revealing ways, some calls for a new understanding of law. Thus, for instance, Mireille Delmas-Marty argues for a "law accessible to all, one not imposed from above like a revealed truth, owned by the official interpreters, but consecrated from the base much like a shared truth, one that is relative and that evolves."[39] Delmas-Marty speaks of a "recomposition d'un paysage" that warrants, in her opinion, a reinvention and ultimately a reinvigoration of common law as she defines it. We can add that this reshaping of the social landscape is, from our perspective, a result of the emerging digital literacy and its effects on the currently established framework for defining and managing intellectual property in the West (but not only in the West) and its social and economic manifestations. The digital environment modifies radically the suppositions as much as the expectations of intellectual property and copyright laws and rules.[40] It does so not only because of the ease with which the technology allows for conversion and transmission of objects but because it fundamentally leads to the dissemination of new practices that are in quest of an appropriate legal framework that recognizes both their legitimacy and their reality. If Delmas-Marty's model for an accessible and shared law makes use of the image of the pyramid in order to illustrate and argue for the necessity for the shift toward a common law (associated with the cloud),[41] it so happens that the cloud has a real and visible digital presence that is tied to some of the features of digital authorship we have been discussing. Tag Clouds are the most obvious manifestation of the distributed anthological authorship; they are decentralized, constantly in flux, and they reflect both the current collective trends while allowing for individual expression. But they also represent a shift in the position and status of the individual in relation to space: a new spatiality, formed by the network and its modalities of presence and its modes of participation, governs the new clouds that are also an expression of the aesthetic of the new digital environment. The image (or the visual), as it has been often argued by critics of the technological society, emanates from a displacement in the form and status of knowledge and its production and cultural consumption. Digital clouds are concentrations of information representing the shifting densities of individual choices shaped by participating in network flux. They are the face of the new collective or, better still, the digital image (in the sense of an active digital object) of the secondary authorship we have characterized as anthological, an authorship that challenges hierarchy and pyramid-like structure, favoring instead evolving participatory models. But it is also important to situate the cloud in aesthetic and structural terms. If, as Damisch argues, the cloud disturbs and undermines the aesthetics of perspective in the Italian Quattrocento, the new digital clouds and their variants are the latest signs of new digital disturbances and their aesthetic, for they incorporate a new spatiality into the socialized network environments. A Tag Cloud is thus more than a collection of pointers; it embodies a semantic density that is characteristically digital. It also gives shape and form to micro-communities that are in the process of defining their identities and their values.

To conclude, the concerns surrounding credibility within Wiki space are not merely a reflection of a struggle between two competing models. They go instead to the core of the long-term viability of authorship as represented by Wikipedia and may shape future participatory knowledge-creation initiatives. They also demonstrate the increasingly political dimension of technological tools and the practices they make possible. The models of the classical city highlighted the spatial and temporal relations between individuals, their identities, and their political communities. They also specified the dynamic intersection between accepted forms of presence and their associated modes of participation, from a variety of increasingly complex and at times difficult to manage forms of representation to a diversity of access to a framework managing privileges and obligations. In a similar fashion, the digital tools and their convergence in socializing practices represent the emergence of new values affecting key notions such as property and its dissemination, individuality, and community. These new values are shaped by ideologies informed by the possibilities or the opportunities that are a direct, and some would argue, natural consequence of a technology that is fundamentally human and communicative. These values are in the last analysis political because they address the relations between individuals and between individuals and their chosen communities. Furthermore, these values blur the lines between the local, the national, the regional, and the global, extending the jurisdictional breakdown occasioned by the distributed nature of the digital environment. The new fuzziness does not lead to a depreciation of the local. On the contrary, the local as well as the global are to be perceived within the new context derived from the emerging social practices. They are to be thought of from the perspective of the emerging political cities. But the digital city is also subject to a fascination with immediacy (the reverse side of presence management) and an obsession with totality. The social network implies, as we will see later on, a willingness to abandon some control over one's own data and to some degree one's identity. It has a utopian dimension that, while political in some of its motivations, is also a function of emerging narrative structures that are the direct result of the new literacy (and its textualtity), and that will play a determining role in forming the new historical archives of the digital environment and its culture. And with the new archives, digital culture will come face to face, in time, with the questions of memory and identity. At this point in time, it would seem that we are only beginning to ask questions concerning the archiving of activities that have become, in principle, fully recordable.[42] For the archive is of our political and social collective memory.

If politics is increasingly shaped to a large measure by access and communication, the digital environment, especially once it matures, is a natural home for politics, for a new politics. If, on the other hand, literacy played a crucial role in shaping modern Western (but not exclusively Western) political practices, how will digital literacy mold the new politics of the future? Free Software and Open Source are the best incarnation of the growing political importance of digital literacy because they challenge our accepted practices concerning intellectual property, commerce, and authorship, and because they are behind most of the tools that are driving the growth of the emerging digital environment. If the city allowed us to visit some of the political dimensions of the digital, Free Software and Open Source are an invitation to walk through its streets and markets.

3

Software Tolerance in the Land of Dissidence

In the previous chapter we considered the continued relevance of frameworks and ideas deeply grounded in the history of print culture, and its legal and political legacy in defining the rules for evaluating digital culture, its innovations, and its potential transformations of our societies. Digital literacy, in the fullest sense of the term, emerges as a key concept in understanding digital culture and, more importantly, in potentially molding new social structures and their political underpinnings, thanks in large part to the ways in which it exploits newer forms of access and exchange of information and knowledge. While still groping with issues concerning credibility and legitimacy, it nevertheless heralds new and, for some, disturbing ways of production and manners of identifying and recognizing property and its ownership. The culture wars focusing on copyright, its extension, and the pressure applied by digital practices on business models for the distribution and exploitation of reproducible works are but one instance of this cultural shift. Our entry point was the city as a model of participatory culture and its political framework. In invoking such a model, we simply recalled some classical formulations without investigating the structure of the modern city and its relations to the emerging digital environment. Thus we did not extend the figure of the city and its opposition to the countryside or the city and its marginal spaces and the ways in which such zones can find echoes within the digital environment itself. Nor did we emphasize the solitary dimension of the city and its capacity for hosting individually determined identities. Instead, we focused on the broadly collective features of the city and its ability to function as a complex site for production: the production of material objects as well as the production of knowledge. The digital city, more universal than any other and more cosmopolitan than its "real life" equivalents, has developed its own geography with its own maps and its own guidance system that go well beyond the mere mirroring of conventional geography, since they call upon (besides the more traditional expectations) the languages and the tools that make the digital environment itself run. In other words, in the digital city, it is increasingly difficult to separate and distinguish the spaces inhabited from the discursive practices that render them possible.

That is so because the culture of digital production goes well beyond the production and distribution of objects: it goes to the core of the digital, namely, the writing and sharing of code. In this case, copyright was a problem from the very early history of digital authorship.[1] This is most visible in the world of Free Software and Open Source,[2] but also, as we have briefly seen, in the changing environment of digital identity and its links with the digital object, and its potential for almost unlimited conversions and transmissions. FOSS provides not only an alternative to the lockup of digital culture and its creations with outdated or inappropriate copyright protections; it puts forward newer models for authoring, creating, and sharing tools and information on a scale unseen before. In other words, FOSS represents the most viable and the most visible picture of the emerging digital culture at work: it offers a rich and at times tumultuous landscape in which individuals and groups collaborate in producing tools that are reliable and sustainable and that are deployed in critical environments while also being accessible to the majority of users. While FOSS has its origin in the divide between traditional copyright and the nature of digital authorship and its objects, it has become the centerpiece for the emerging digital literacy and the environment it is creating. But it has also become the focus of an important conflict between established corporate and commercial interests firmly grounded in the tradition of intellectual property protections and the emerging business and social models shaped by the distributed participatory models of FOSS. In this sense, FOSS allows us to examine closely the differences between two divergent economics of literacy (print and digital) and to think about some of the implications of the continued success and spread of the FOSS authoring paradigm, its legal ramifications, and its broader cultural dimensions.

I. Universality and Tolerance: A Digital Convergence?

It is customary, when discussing the current digital politics, to oppose FOSS to Closed Source, Closed Source referring mostly to software that is delivered exclusively in binary form without allowing the user any access to the source code or granting him any rights to modify it: in other words, the divide between Closed and Open centers on the nature of the digital object itself and on the limits set by the authors (or producers and distributors) as to the rights of users to manipulate the digital object. While this initial opposition reveals the intimate ties between the production of digital objects and the current state of our expectations about the distribution and use of intellectual property, it fails to give a full and accurate picture of the extent of the divide between Closed and Open Source models. It fails in part, because it privileges the representation of FOSS (and we will discuss shortly some of the differences between the Free and Open models) as a deviation from the established norm, and because it retains its identification as a dissident movement that seeks to challenge the legitimacy of Closed Source. While indeed it is true that Free Software, and later on Open Source, emerged from the recognition of the need for an alternative to the Closed Source controls over the basic tools of the digital environment, FOSS was and remains a cultural movement with its own ideology and beliefs. It is my contention in this chapter that FOSS is not a deviation from the established and now challenged norm, but instead it is, if such a term is at all applicable in the digital environment, *natural* in the sense that it is most appropriate to the nature and qualities of the digital object itself. In order to appreciate this characteristic of Free and Open Source, I will describe its difference from Closed Source by calling on a simple religious model, one that opposes orthodoxy and heresy. If I chose this religious model, it is in part because the difference between FOSS and Closed Source reflects radically divergent attitudes toward belief and digital literacy: each, as we shall see, is a site (or, in some cases, sites) for emerging narratives about the role and status of belief systems, values, and ethics of authorship and citizenship in the digital environment. The religious model allows us to evaluate the significance of credibility[3] in the digital age, and along with it the ways in which digital culture, with its own emerging nexus of problems, addresses concerns about responsibility and accountability. Credibility, in this instance, pertains to the modalities of conversion of some of the essential social and cultural categories (from privacy to security and identity, to name only a few) into their digital incarnations and the processes with which such a conversion is currently being negotiated. In other words, the credibility we are discussing here has to do with the juridical status of the digital object, its creation and mode of production, and its distribution and reproduction.

Tolerance, in the technical environment, refers to the ability of systems to integrate fault management. In other words, technical or technological tolerance stands for a design system that acknowledges error and one that is meant to correct such errors. This is not what I mean by software tolerance in this chapter. Instead, I would like to propose the religious and social notion of tolerance for the software. In other words, I would like to extend the model we have come to accept as essential for our conception and our understanding of civil harmony to the field of software understood in the broadest possible terms. Software in this case is not restricted to the code or to its often complex authorship: it also covers the practices it generates and the extensions and conversions it makes possible. In brief, software provides the underlying support for the digital environment and its literacy. In effect, the current digital landscape, while exhibiting normalizing tendencies, remains the locus of difference and dissidence. It has retained the pioneering spirit of discovery and innovation and has managed change and convergence while supporting and often valuing the marginal if not the eccentric. Within the digital landscape we see a tension between the drive toward a universal thrust and the continuous emergence of dissenting and eccentric voices and spaces. Such a tension is best observed when one examines censorship on a national scale or when analyzing the globalization of tools and their conflict with local cultures and protocols. This is simply to point out that software tolerance is perhaps a better name for what we have so far termed the digital divide, for it covers the problems raised by access (access to the network and access to digital objects and to the rights to manipulate them), those related to conversion (conversion from print to digital, conversion between different and at times competing formats, and conversion between tools), and the issues raised by digital identity and digital forms of authorship.

Tolerance, it goes without saying, is a historical category. In our Western culture, it is intimately related to religious history, and it emerged into a significant social and ultimately political category in the early Modern period. But tolerance has its roots in dissidence, or more precisely in heresy. How do we accept difference in religious and doctrinal opinion? The conflict between the universal (we would today say global) and the different constitutes the core of tolerance. The dynamic between orthodoxy and heresy or between a monolithic and relatively stable and unchanging fixed universality[4] (in digital terms, we would say a monolithic culture) and an ever-changing variation and conversion defines the process of formation of tolerance and its translation into a basis for social and political protections of freedoms. It is my contention that, at least for the time being, FOSS plays the role of heresy or heresies in the face of Closed Source (understood as not only a model for the production and distribution of code but also as the legal framework that perpetuates inherited conceptions of authorship and intellectual property protections derived from print culture and extended to the digital age). In order to give the reader an idea about the differences between the orthodox and the heretical, we can point to a series of texts written at the end of the seventeenth century that tried to define the meaning and the history of both orthodoxy and heresy. The orthodox or Catholic position was perhaps best articulated by Jacques-Bénigne Bossuet, in his polemical *Histoire des variations des églises protestantes* (1688), for whom the Catholic position is universal and therefore accepts no variation from the official orthodoxy, whereas the Protestant (whom Bossuet calls the heretic) is someone who prefers his own opinion to that of the Church. The Protestants themselves, arguing for a healthy diversity, were represented by individuals like Leibniz (*The Theodicy*, published in 1710) and Pierre Bayle (*Dictionnaire historique et critique* [1697]).[5] For them, the heretic (heresy is derived from the Greek *haireomai, eligo, I choose*) represents a healthy tolerance and the freedom of choice. To summarize, Catholic universality is viable only through a single, centralized organization, whereas Protestant diversity gets its vitality from the proliferation of interrelated yet slightly different groups. The difference between the universal and the heretic is one that is mirrored in the most common critique of FOSS: its diversity and fragmentation and the ensuing lack of coherence and continuity.

Closed Source offerings accept only minor variations: in operating systems, Windows and Apple OS X (although there exists an Open Source version of Apple, called Darwin) are good examples. Almost every aspect of the system is controlled and subject to a rather restrictive license. On the other hand, a quick look at DistroWatch or SourceForge testifies to the rich diversity of the FOSS movement and its offerings.[6] But the similarities between the debates around tolerance in the early Modern period and the current struggle over the control of the desktop go well beyond this initially simple analogy.

FOSS ideology, as we shall see shortly, grounded in an international, communal effort, relies on flexible conceptions of freedom and responsibility (it resembles another relatively "heretical" modern religious movement, Liberation Theology).[7] Closed Source delivers a unique, uniform, and universal product that is supposed to satisfy all needs across cultures. It also, and this is the crucial difference, tries to restrict access to its environment from any other system, to the extent possible. Closed Source, to use our earlier terminology, is written mostly for passive "users" or consumers. In other words, in religious terms, it is not ecumenical in its behavior despite its claims to universality. Closed Source, according to my simplified model, is Catholic whereas FOSS, in its diversity, is essentially Protestant.

Recent trends and developments in Digital Rights Management and the Initiative for Software Choice make the analogy even more relevant. It is once again time to argue strongly, in order to protect the rights of users, for the separation of church and state: the government adoption of laws against piracy is inspired by further Closed Source corporate objectives under the guise of copyright and intellectual property protection (DVDs with their DRM and regional controls are but one example). This is particularly relevant since the arguments put forward to support Closed Source efforts to manage users' desktops (and now their online presence) are based on the presumed economic impact of piracy. Yet, it is generally accepted that economic growth in the Modern period was brought forth by the rise and proliferation of Protestant ("heretical") sects and their intellectual vitality.[8]

Before examining in some more detail the genesis of FOSS and its current state, some questions that will have to be addressed from the point of view of software tolerance include: What will be the impact of the rise of FOSS as an epistemological model on the evolution of the digital environment, and how will an operating system such as Asianux (if it is adopted)[9] initiative play into the growing conflict between divergent national conceptions of intellectual property and collaborative systems? How will the notion of "property" and authorship be modified if not redefined by the rising popularity and adoption of FOSS models and methods? Will the opposition between a monoculture (Closed Source) and a diverse platform translate into a political reality? If tolerance, in a technological context, implies taking account of and managing errors within the digital environment, software tolerance calls for a more enlightened and informed acceptance of software production and discursive practices that not only highlight the current shortcomings of our legal framework when it comes to managing intellectual property and cultural productions in the digital age, but also pave the way for new economic realities embedded within digital practices. The recent Viacom lawsuit against Google and YouTube shows the growing difficulty of separating current practices from theoretically illegal or suspect activities. For instance, the common practice of being able to restrict access to online posted material is seen by copyright holders as merely a strategy to hide illegal material.[10] And yet, such a practice pertains to both privacy (family access, etc.) and, in my opinion, more importantly, to the nature of the technology itself. In other words, the print model of intellectual property and copyright cannot but restrict and constrain uses that are simply natural within the digital environment. A draconian interpretation would argue that in fact current corporate copyright holders aim precisely to contain digital practices in order to better

extend their current business models without any regard to the technological reality.

II. Schisms and Literate Markets

The conflict between FOSS and Closed Source, while initially restricted
to operating systems, has now spread to cover the full range of digital technology, from formats of digital objects to access to content, and more recently to distributed Web-based digital presence. In other words, what was
in the beginning a difference pertaining to the role of copyright protections and the distribution of code has nowadays become a generalized divergence about the nature of digital production and the role to be played by
users within the digital environment itself. It even extends to journalism
with the rise of "citizen journalism" and the difficult transition, for most
printed press, into the digital environment.

   Free Software is perhaps the purest form of digital dissidence to emerge
early in the digital era.[11] It represents a movement that has played and
continues to play an essential role in the evolution of the digital environment, if only due to the importance of the Copyleft movement and the
GPL.[12] It is, in a sense, the model for most of the current variations from
Open Source to the Creative Commons, to name only two of the most
representative movements. But what are the principal characteristics of
Free Software? In essence, Free Software tries to harmonize four instances of freedom with the realities of the digital environment and digital technology. It is an ethical movement that is grounded in a form of
responsibility that does not curtail or restrict the inherent freedom of the
digital itself. From our perspectives, it can be safely said that the four
freedoms (the freedom to run a program, the freedom to have access to the
inner workings of the program, the freedom to redistribute code, and
the freedom to modify a program)[13] are ultimately based on the nature
of the digital object and on digital literacy itself. In this context, Copyleft
(the right to package and distribute code under rules that respect and protect the four freedoms) represents a pragmatic idealism, or a departure
from the norms of established copyright and intellectual property protections that ultimately challenge the continued relevance and intelligibility
of the customary acceptance of ownership. Free Software takes its radical

point of departure from the full realization of the radicality of the digital object itself and the specificity of forms of authorship it calls for and encourages. While contesting the validity of an economic and political model based on ownership, it introduces software (understood as the authoring and literate use of code) as a new cultural model, as the new icon for digital culture.

Open Source, while the heir to Free Software (and at times its rival), also grew out of a reflection on the models of authoring and production of code and their analysis. Its founding essay opposes, at least in its most defining image, two models of social hierarchies and exchange, the Cathedral and the Bazaar.[14] The now classic opposition between the Cathedral and the Bazaar incorporates an opposition to religious forms of hierarchy and its controls over production and exchange between individuals and creators. The Cathedral, a pyramid-like structure that bestows meaning and significance from higher authority, protects homogeneity and ultimately, in our terms, orthodoxy. It leads to the perpetual management of change and innovation from the perspective of an established authority, an authority that, by its very essence, seeks to reproduce itself and to propagate its own image. For us, the Bazaar is an environment that encourages the spread and the development of digital literacy. In Eric Raymond's essay, the opposition between the Cathedral and the Bazaar initially stands for the difference between two development models, one commercial and the second free or open (Linux). Two basic problems emerge from the comparison: first, how to best manage the growing complexity of the digital tools to be produced, and then how to evaluate the economic implications of each model.

Raymond qualifies the Bazaar by the proliferation of seemingly competing and at times conflicting "styles." In fact, it would seem that the Bazaar is inhabited by conflictual opinions and schools, by a plurality qualified as a Babel (and its confusion of languages), and generally by a series of metaphors and images that all convey, on first look, a confusion, a lack of direction and of order, and an absence of a clear objective and guidance. The Cathedral offers an authoritative and a centralized management of production goals and methods whereas the Bazaar thrives on "styles" and expands, thanks to its "promiscuity"; these traits, over time, lead to new production models. Promiscuity is but a name for tolerance, software tolerance, an informed tolerance that is inclusive while maintaining quality controls: an inclusive tolerance, in the sense that while it discriminates for quality, it nevertheless continuously invites greater and improved collaboration. The styles that circulate in the Bazaar explain its "anthological" nature: it is, in a sense, the site of a degree zero of the digital authorship and its literacy. It relies on reuse or rewriting. It is an active model for the transmission and management of inherited code. Its legacy is that it makes material otherwise inaccessible available to all and everyone. Ultimately, "promiscuity" or software tolerance works because it is a creative displacement, an ongoing reorientation. It innovates because of its anthological nature: it is a process of modification and extension. It is a literate engagement with predecessors. The Ancients are constantly becoming Moderns. Circulation of code as well as of practices makes for a sustainable model of digital authorship. The Bazaar suffers, in my opinion, from the eminence of the marketplace as the defining metaphor. What is perhaps needed is an emphasis not only on the competitive pressures that are supposed to produce improved software or journalism, but a closer appreciation of the discursive practices that the Bazaar invites: a multiplicity that at times borders, for some, on cacophony; a diversity that appears to be destined to produce small, splintered divisions and schisms. In this perspective, Free Software is ultimately more suited to the nature of the digital environment and the digital object itself, although the Open Source movement has succeeded in remarkable ways.

III. A Digital Vulgate, Its Common Places and Eloquence

This brief description of Free Software and Open Source is meant to highlight FOSS as a cultural movement with social, political, and of course technological consequences that have come to shape an important proportion of our current digital landscape. While its origins may lie in the desire to provide a framework that is essentially free and unencumbered by any copyright and intellectual property controls and restrictions, it has evolved along with the digital environment itself, offering not only some of its most essential and basic tools (Internet protocols to name only the most obvious) but also influencing our expectations and forming our practices about our presence and our status in digital culture. It has transformed technology into a literate form, and this increasing literacy is best illustrated by the changes in the digital environment itself. We have slowly but surely come to accept and embrace free and open access to larger and richer online tools and activities, and ultimately, to an assumption of openness about the nature of online presence and information, and the role we choose to play in the digital environment. If the early history of FOSS is inseparable from a choice and an attitude that are first expressed by a legal document or documents (a license), this history showcases the divide between print and digital (and their fundamentally distinct juridical assumptions). Its evolution encapsulates the struggle to define the nature of work in the digital age, of its value and methods of valuation, and of the ethical and political implications of such a choice. Thus it is not in the least surprising to encounter the FOSS model in variations throughout the currently expanding frontiers of the digital environment. But beyond the intimate intertwining of the Free and Open models and digital culture itself, it is instructive to look into the ways in which the resulting practices are inevitably transforming some of our most basic cultural and social categories.

FOSS is, in a sense, an expression, in digital terms, of our relations with our past and its authorities. It is, in other words, an instance of rare conceptual shifts, compressed into a relatively brief span of time, unfolding before us. It is *visible* to all, and anyone who has access is by definition a potential player and participant. Its schismatic or heretical nature makes it inclusive: it offers a choice by choosing to be open to those who can read in the digital sense of the term. And precisely because of its inclusive tendency, FOSS functions as a great agent for the advancement and spread of digital literacy. For as we have seen, underlying its conception of freedom and openness we find the requisite digital authorship itself. Access to code implies readability but also an expectation of adaptation: the user is already a coder, and the reader already an author, whether such an extension applies to simple or cosmetic modifications of the look and feel of an application or a site, or whether it involves important modifications, adaptations, and extensions of code snippets. In all such cases, FOSS is the engine behind the new Vulgate, or the proliferation of, to paraphrase Dante, the vulgar digital languages.[15] FOSS desacralizes digital technology: it insists on the importance of its accessibility, at all possible levels, to humans, to the human eye as much as to the individual as a potential author. It is therefore not in the least surprising that FOSS, while giving rise to powerful and successful environments, always produces an increasing diversity of choices that can appear confusing, if not ultimately futile. To stay with Dante for one more moment, the dissident nature of FOSS, its Babel-like structure, much like the diversity of human languages and their apparent confusion, has its own eloquence. Such diversity, much like the proliferation of "heresies" in earlier periods, testifies to the vitality of the movement and to its potential for continuous fragmentation, a fragmentation that is in my opinion insurmountable.

In what follows, while loosely using the orthodoxy/heresy divide to discuss FOSS and the ways in which it provides an impetus toward continuous change in the digital environment, we will look into some of the most representative areas of digital culture affected by its influence. It will be important to keep in mind the difference between FOSS (and in this case especially Open Source) as a cultural movement inherent to digital culture and Open Source as an effort to legitimize FOSS as a business model. While it is true, as I have pointed out earlier, that FOSS, by its very nature, poses serious challenges to established norms and models for economic valuation and compensation, my main focus in this chapter is the cultural movement behind such challenges and its interventions in the general realm of knowledge production and exchange in the digital environment. In other words, our objective here is the conceptual displacements operated by FOSS in the general arena of culture, from the relations between citizens and their governments to the emerging social networks and their impact on identity, and finally to the spread and complexification of digital literacy.[16] Ultimately, we will be discussing a convergence between forms of authorship, production values, and digital social environments (in the broadest sense of the term), and their political and economic dimensions. It is as if, in the final analysis, the new digital landscape is being molded to a large degree by the FOSS model, by the tools it is producing and the culture of sharing and distributing that support it. In this perspective, the recent trends in social networking toward a diversified partition based on intersecting interests and values mirrors the variety of FOSS schools and models. In these cases, the social in social networking is both a cultural manifestation and a technological practice. It is at the same time a business model and a way to produce and to share in an increasingly literate fashion. Still, it is important to note that while FOSS appears often as an agency of change and a departure from past models, it is in fact the site of permanence and of continuity. Not only has it been around since the earliest ages of the digital era; it has also evolved in a manner that tends to both secure access to the digital and ensure the acceptance of digital culture itself. In short, it is our Vulgate, and as such it grows and advances thanks to tolerance and by furthering tolerance, by extending the notion of tolerance to what is most radically digital—code and its production and distribution.

DabbleDB, a recent Web site that aims to bring the social networking and some of the Web 2.0 user-generated content models to the realm of codes, illustrates clearly this evolution.[17] While the main site is commercial and requires a paid account, the company also offers an Open Source version of its services, called DabbleDB Commons, in which users can upload and share their codes in order to make them available to other users. In this case, all code is visible and accessible to everyone.[18] Such a site affords us a number of insights. First, it actualizes what has been common for some time in the world of software development, and especially the ever-popular scripting languages, namely, the growing importance of reusable code and its portability. We can describe this phenomenon as a natural evolution, within the current state of the digital environment, of the ideal of Object Oriented programming languages, into the broader area of what we may term Web OS. Second, it formalizes the departure from the secret models of development of application into the recognition of a shared code base that, while public, does not necessarily preclude or weaken innovation and creativity. Thus we move from secrecy or private development to a participatory culture of social competition.

While initially the site attracts programmers, it is very easy to see that it can also appeal to the users who are not afraid of trying their hand at some programming, since most of the available code is easily deployable on blogs and personal Web sites or via some of the more popular Web APIs (maps, etc.). Here we witness the convergence of a programming model (Object Oriented) and of FOSS that results in the extension of the Free and Open model to include not only content but also the creation of digital tools. The anthological turn is obviously at work here, for we see that code or objects are thought of as fragments in the sense of snippets that are autonomous and self-contained and that are designed to be inserted and to function in a diversity of environments and contexts. The anthological characterizes not only the user experience in the digital environment, but it also plays an increasingly important role in the authoring of tools that are constantly transforming it. Code objects are the digital equivalents of classical "common places" that are the highlight of its rhetoric and eloquence, and their increasing accessibility is but a symptom of the evolution of digital literacy.

I think what is most important about such dynamic aggregation of resources is the inseparability of code and content and the collapse of the differences between authors and readers or between coders and users, and the ultimate transformation of usability by access and accessibility. Access to content and access to the objects that allow for the manipulation and transformation of content: such is the work of digital literacy and the openness it requires. Code and its social usability provide the foundations for a literate market, a market of object and of ideas, a market for the deployment of the emerging values of digital culture. The key terms for these values, as we shall see, are openness and access, understood in a broad enough sense to cover their potential in the digital environment.

IV. Software and Political Representation

Before discussing some of the most representative movements behind Open Access in its diversity and copyright reform, we need to look briefly into the structure of FOSS and its legal status. By this I mean not the status of Free Software and Open Source licenses and their validity, but instead the legal problems raised by FOSS as a cultural model for the production of code and knowledge. If FOSS represents the heretical tendency we have briefly described, its legal position is nothing more than a sheer absence. In fact, one of the difficulties facing FOSS derives from the questions surrounding its fluid authorship and the manner in which it makes it difficult to assign responsibility. Perhaps the best illustration of this is part of the story of the DVD Copy Control Association's CSS or Content Scrambling Scheme.[19] Since the CSS was designed to be licensed to hardware makers and content distributors, it, from the beginning, excluded Linux as a legitimate participant, because Linux as an operating system is not produced by any single legal entity (although there are companies that can sell a specific distribution). In other words, in the case of Hollywood's protection of its entertainment content, it did not recognize Linux or any of its derivatives as a valid interlocutor or partner. For indeed, who can speak for the FOSS community? Who is authorized to do so and what are the mechanisms for such an authorization and recognition? Thus, it would seem that the absence of a recognizable if not unified legal representation (and in this case legal is a synonym for commercial) amounts to an exclusion that leads immediately to illegality. Users of Linux have but two choices: either they try to purchase a license to gain access to content, or they try to circumvent such a protection. What matters for us here is the fact that current legal framework does not yet have a place for Linux as an operating system or for the majority of FOSS-produced software. It would seem that the heretical nature of the movement destines it for the margins of legality.

The situation of FOSS vis-à-vis CSS reminds us of a Greek story told by Porphyry in his *De Abstinentia*.[20] After a crime, no one was able to identity the murderer. All those who were present or who were assumed to be somehow connected to the murder were convoked to a gathering to try to elucidate the mystery. All were present, including the knife with which the murder was committed. Each of the present individuals denied any responsibility for the crime and at the end, the silent party, the knife, was recognized as the guilty party. Silence is equated with guilt, and FOSS, as the de facto silent party in the legal debates surrounding access to content, is often assumed to be such a guilty party. Much like the knife, FOSS as a set of tools and technologies is not recognized as a legal person and is therefore kept out of the negotiations, although there can be obvious agreements between companies producing and distributing FOSS software and Multimedia or any other content distributors. The case of CSS is instructive because it highlights the limitations of the current legal framework in its efforts to manage the emerging digital practices and the need for a reevaluation of the processes with which copyright laws are not only formulated but also enforced. Furthermore, the extension of the FOSS model, especially into the domain of online sharing of multimedia material, will only increase the pressure to either tighten abusively restrictive controls that can radically impoverish users' experience or to revisit altogether the inherited model from print culture and all of its assumptions and constructs. But beyond such a condition, the question remains as to the representation of Free Software and Open Source not as a single product or tool, but as a movement and a culture. How do we take into account a production model that cannot be tied to a single author or to a single group, a model that is by essence anthological and cumulative and that brings together individuals and groups based in different locations and therefore that come under different jurisdictions? In short, how do we make the silence of FOSS speak?

While there are currently new efforts (which we will look into shortly) that are trying to remedy some of the difficulties raised by the peculiar nature of FOSS from a legal point of view, the situation we are faced with here is an eloquent illustration of a dimension of the digital divide we discussed briefly earlier. Rarely have we seen in recent times an issue with such a broad impact legislated with as much ignorance, in part because legislative bodies (the United States and France are two prime examples here) have, whether willingly or not, chosen to ignore the larger picture in their proceedings, focusing instead on local or narrowly defined problems pertaining to copyright and the status of the author, privacy or even digital security. While it can be easily argued that the legislative and the political process work in this fashion (and here, once again, FOSS still lacks a powerful enough voice), and therefore it is unrealistic to expect a change in the case of digital technology, we would counter by pointing out, with many other critics and observers, that these legislations have always resulted in potential modifications to the most common digital practices, and therefore have been rarely successful. It is so because the legislators are either unfamiliar with digital culture or because they choose to maintain print as the defining model for all intellectual property rights and management. Thus we are constantly faced with a rhetoric of piracy or the protection of authors and creators, a rhetoric that, while at times well-meaning, tends in effect to defend the interest of groups and/or corporations that continue to resist the changes brought about by digital literacy. The legislative divide can also lead to a more serious divide, one that increasingly creates conflict between rich and developed countries and poorer and underdeveloped nations. As a case in point, one can point to the growing efforts by the United States to tie economic agreement and aid to copyright and intellectual property laws in foreign countries. Financial cooperation or aid is thus tied to a misguided set of laws that are often contested and challenged at home.

But what matters most is the fact that laws that are designed to manage the digital environment have become economic and political tools for national governments; they have been transformed into bargaining chips in financial and diplomatic negotiations. And they are so in order, in part, to stem the adoption of FOSS models, because these models threaten the stability of the copyright and intellectual property edifice. In other words, the effort to export copyright laws amounts to an effort to export its assumptions. So far, we can safely say that the political class as a group has failed to grasp the scale and radicality of the changes brought about by digital culture: it continues to think of the digital, despite its all-too-apparent difference and autonomy, as a mere *extension* of the past, and therefore laws need to be made more precise in order to take note of the current situation, while it is rather evident that the practices adopted in the digital environment challenge directly some of the key assumptions of print and its elaborate legal culture. I am far from arguing for an absolute, radical form of change. Instead, I am simply calling for an informed realism that respects the features of the digital environment and an enlightened pragmatism that is lucid enough to see the need for a serious rethinking of copyright and intellectual property in the digital age.

If FOSS lacks any viable representation, it is nonetheless not completely silent. It speaks loudly and clearly thanks to the millions of users who every day participate in sites and online activities, validating its cultural appeal. If, in our Greek tale of murder and responsibility, silence was synonymous with guilt, or to be more precise, silence was interpreted by a group of individuals as a sign of guilt, we are led to wonder why legislative bodies and some worldwide organizations are incapable of hearing and registering the sounds of their citizens. In the tale, the knife is a tool, it is the agency of bloodletting, it is an object that makes it possible to kill. It is tempting to extend the analogy between the knife and FOSS; each is conspicuous by its silence, and yet each shapes the legal process. And yet, what distinguishes the two is that they do not speak the current common language. In the case of the knife, it is mute. In the case of FOSS, it speaks a new language, one that has not yet entered the domain of public legisla-tion. Most FOSS tools are the product of neither a company nor a recog-nizable and localizable entity. The knife stands for a reality that was al-ways present but not necessarily recognized. It speaks violence thorough silence. FOSS is not only a set of growing technologies or development en-vironments and Linux distribution; it provides the framework for a literate and accessible digital environment; it offers access to digital literacy instead of managing and controlling the distribution of digital objects. It repre-sents the swelling voices of the new literate classes in quest of a political voice.[21]

V. Licensing Babel, or Open Orthodoxy

Our starting analogy in this chapter was a religion, exploiting the dynam-ics between orthodoxy and heresy and the conflict between the supposed benefits of a unified and homogeneous environment, and the potential dangers of fragmentation represented by the tendency of heresy to gener-ate ever-smaller groups and increasing divisions. Indeed, in this perspec-tive, we may consider the large number of Linux distributions as a reflec-tion of such a condition and one in which these distributions (which are all variations of two paradigmatic models, Red Hat and Debian) as the equiv-alent to Confessions, in the sense that they articulate minor deviation or adaptations of their founding models.[22] One is tempted to speak of a true experience of religious variety in the digital realm, where belief is trans-lated into the choice of an operating system or of a license. But while dis-tributions are perhaps the most visible manifestation of FOSS's richness and seemingly endless proliferation, what may be more significant and more powerful considering the growing efforts to control intellectual property due to the pressure of digital practices, is the growth of licenses in the Free Software and Open Source world. In this context, the prolif-eration of either distributions (or operating systems) and licenses ex-presses the increasingly participatory nature of the digital environment and the evolution of the model of choice it makes available. Licenses thus express more than a fragmentary environment and its particular eccen-tricities: they instead capture the diversity of experiences and orientations in a changing market where ideas and their digital incarnations shape the economics as much as the social dimensions of the digital environment. Furthermore, the growth of licenses is also driven by the popularity of new services and tools that integrate and automate licensing of user-generated content.[23]

In today's digital landscape, it would seem that licenses, at least in the FOSS world, are roughly divided between content and software, with licensing schemes shared by both categories. It is perhaps instructive to recall that in the early stages of the digital era, when software was exclusively hardware specific, it was offered for free as part of the purchase of a machine. At the time when computers were more expensive and almost the sole realm of corporations, government agencies, and universities and research institutions, computers were accessible to a relatively few, expert users.[24] But with the shift to a networked environment and the personal PC, licensing schemes became essential as software was divorced from hardware and became of value in and of itself. In other words, with the evolution of the digital environment from a computational framework into, in theory, a literate culture open and available to all, we moved from a context in which software was not considered an autonomous and valued product on its own to a condition in which it has become almost more important than the machine itself. It is such a shift (that is both economic and cultural) from a reliance on hardware to a valuation of practices driven exclusively (from the perspective of users) by software that explains the rise in licensing schemes and the current divide between FOSS and Closed Software camps. Thus it is fair to say that the complex landscape that is the digital environment currently is shaped by the determining role played by users and their drive toward increasing exchange and sharing of tidbits of information or of self-generated content in distributed environments. Licenses, especially FOSS licenses, accompany and enhance the advancement of digital literacy: they are in effect its expression in both practical and legal terms. And, in a similar fashion, the licenses testify to changes brought about by what has been called the *Interface Culture* (the move from Command Line and the current dominance of the Web interface, i.e., the browser).[25] Interface Culture is important because it made possible the general adoption of computing skills and thus paved the way for digital literacy. But Interface Culture also has its history, and this history relates to the genesis of licenses and the role played by Unix.

In fact, the two most important and most popular original Free Software licenses are related to Unix and its copyright protections. Both the Berkeley System Distribution (BSD) and the GPL have common origins in that they both aimed at producing, or better still at converting, the Unix operating system into copyright free code.[26] While BSD has its roots in academic research, the GPL grew not only out of a desire to produce an equivalent to Unix but also the realization of the need to protect the code from potential proprietary appropriations. Thus, BSD never restricted any potential commercial use, whereas the GPL included the clause that protected its conversion offering of open and free code from proprietary and commercial modifications. The BSD license is one of the most permissive, whereas the GPL registers copyright and adds to it controls over the specific terms of distribution in order to explicitly shield the further distribution and modification of the code. While both licenses grew out of efforts to make Unix-compatible tools and libraries, what is relevant to our current situation and our discussions here is the ways in which each chose to represent freedom: the freedom to use the code, the freedom to modify it, and the conditions under which such modifications may be redistributed.

While both licenses are initially linked to Unix, they have become, since the rise of Interface Culture and the spread of current digital technology, models for thinking not only about code and its distribution but also about the notion of access itself as an expression of a fundamental freedom in the digital environment: access to information, access to the network, and access to the building blocks that make the environment what it is. In a strong sense, they furnished, along with related efforts that developed after the spread of personal computing and the consequent transformation of the digital landscape, the initial shell for digital literacy. Thus, as we shall shortly see, the Free and Open model will spread to almost every aspect of information and material that can be made available and accessed online, from research and scholarly publications, to user-generated content. There are currently at least sixty Free and Open licenses and remarkably enough, this diversity does not hamper the continued development and success of Free and Open Source software.[27] For some, especially for defenders of strict intellectual property controls and producers of Closed Source applications, this diversity is nothing but a Babel that reflects the confusion of the FOSS world and its inability to provide a clear and stable legal framework for digital products. And yet, with the success of major platforms and services as well as a growing realization of the need for coherent and Open Access strategies to all aspects of digital culture, we can say that this Babel, like proliferation of licenses, is a sign of a healthy evolution, one that signals a fundamental shift in which the heretical movement represented by the Free and Open Software is slowly but surely becoming the orthodoxy in the digital age, but an Open Orthodoxy, one that is firmly grounded in an philosophy of Free and Open Access. This shift has radical consequences for every activity related to the production of knowledge and its distribution in the digital age, from scientific and scholarly publishing to government's role in managing access to such information, to the production of the next generation of tools and applications, and finally to the status of user-generated content and its circulation on the network. In other words, this shift will play a central role in shaping the next-stage general economy of the digital environment.

It is important to note, however, that the majority of these licenses are written in American English and are initially based on U.S. copyright law and its language and traditions, and while they have been translated into a large number of languages, not all of these translations are adaptations to national laws and customs. However, this situation has changed recently with the emergence of national efforts to adapt the text and the spirit of the major FOSS licenses into national documents.[28] In other words, the licensing Babel is also slowly becoming available in all of the other languages, but its translation is also a sign of cultural diversity and adaptations that register, in their versions of the license, the specificities of each local context, its history, and its customs. Furthermore, this slow migration from American English reflects both the spread of digital literacy and the increasing importance of content in the new digital environment, for most of the licenses now address the protections and access and modification and distribution rules governing either directly created digital content or existing content made available for the first time on the network. Thus, a quick survey of the licenses shows the emergence of licenses that cover, for instance, documentation; ones that are exclusively devoted to artistic works; and others that concern themselves with broadly defined content of all sorts.[29]

Perhaps a good indication of the political potential of this shift is to be found in the recently published Rapport Rocard, prepared on the occasion of the French presidential elections, but one whose content goes beyond mere campaigning.[30] Revealingly, the proposal is entitled *République 2.0*, signaling the influence of the latest trends in the digital environment on the political discourse for innovation and change vis-à-vis digital technology. But what the proposal calls for that is directly relevant to our concerns here is, in fact, the adoption of a balanced Open Access model that, while guaranteeing protections of copyright and intellectual property, recognizes the new reality of the digital environment and its digital literacy. Thus:

> Users have been endowed by the new digital tools with immensely enlarged capacity to copy, exchange, recommend works, to express themselves and finally to create their own works. The frontier clearly separating user from creator has become hazy, and creators of new cultural content can envisage new possibilities for reaching extensive publics and thus for rejuvenating their works.
>
> The traditional cultural industries are faced with the choice either of maintaining the commercial models that they developed to make war on their own users or of adapting to the new cultural practices at the price of a drastic modification of their present commercial models. We need to help them to work through this transition, especially the independent producers, without ever losing sight of the fact that this transition is inevitable.[31]

Indeed, taking into account a key feature of digital literacy and its implications for a cultural policy is essential if we are to avoid the culture wars and the conflict between traditional cultural and entertainment industry and the current digital practices. In this context, the concepts of Free and Open Access represented by the FOSS licenses are at the core of the shift from the traditional, print-inspired model for culture and its legal and financial support, and thus become unavoidable for any enlightened discussion of national or cultural policy regarding artistic creation and intellectual property in the digital era. Before looking into Open Access,[32] especially in its relation to scholarly and scientific publishing, we need to conclude our survey of FOSS licenses and their relation to digital literacy with a discussion of Creative Commons licenses, if only because of their success, especially with the Web 2.0 platforms, from services like Flickr and Blogger.

Creative Commons licenses are, once again, a product of American legal culture and its confrontation with the digital era.[33] They reflect the convergence of thinking about the public domain (and the trend to restrict it because of abusive extensions of copyright terms and protections) and the emerging digital practices. Thus, taking the lead from the Free Software Foundation's initial GPL license, Creative Commons formulated legally valid and digitally appropriate licenses that are specifically designed for products that are not software, but are instead cultural and digital products such as Web sites, blogs, films, literature, and so on.[34] What is perhaps unique about Creative Commons licenses is their digital nature: while they are legally valid licenses, they are also digital objects themselves, objects that are embedded within Web sites or blogs, or that are attached to a variety of digital objects (photos, films, etc.). In other words, they were thought out and conceived from within the digital environment and its tools and thus they were, from the beginning, integrated with digital practices. The licenses come in three forms: a Commons Deed, that is to say, a common language summary of the legal license itself, understandable by nonlegal experts; a Legal Code, or the technical text of the license itself; and finally, and more importantly from our point of view, a Digital Code of the license. The Digital Code is significant because, first, it allows for the production of a machine-readable version of the license, thus making it available to search engines and to other tools that can query, analyze, and point to digital objects associated with a specific license. The Digital Code version of the license also makes it possible to inform users as to what kind of protections are given to material or content as they browse, thanks to the integration of Creative Commons. In this case, Creative Commons has provided the first fully digital licenses and has thus managed an essential part of the transition from the current copyright customs into the digital environment. For, beyond merely shaping the user's experience by revealing the licenses attached to particular sites or specific content, they also make the case for the need of specific forms of licensing that are adapted to the realities of digital culture and its tools.

In the same vein, Creative Commons provides a further service toward the maturing of digital literacy by making accessible to the largest possible number of users and creators the act of licensing itself. Thus, its relatively simple but effective scheme for choosing a license makes it easy to generate valid and digitally available licenses for almost anyone online. The basic model has four categories of choice, and each license depends on what combination of options is selected by the user. The categories are Attribution (whether the creator chooses to require acknowledgment as part of the distribution of a work), Commercial (or Noncommercial, or whether the user allows for commercial adaptation of a work), Derivative Works (whether or not modifications are allowed), and finally Sharing (whether to Share Alike or not, i.e., whether to extend the kind of license to derivative works). The four categories are basic abstractions of the intersections and the interface between what is easily possible in the digital environment and the potential protections under copyright laws. In other words, Creative Commons combines standard and customary digital manipulations of objects with their respective legal expression and protections. But it also does much more than that: it gives users the choice to contribute to enriching the public domain by making their creations available to others under terms of their choice, and terms that are digitally as well as legally readable and valid. In short, Creative Commons is the digital manifestation of the idealist or the Advancement of Knowledge and Science wing of U.S. copyright law (as opposed to the Utilitarian wing, which tends to emphasize the need of stronger protections for the sake of financial benefits for creators).[35] In this respect, the divide between the "Progress of Science" and the Utilitarian interpretations is symptomatic of the overall crisis in copyright and intellectual property brought about by emerging digital practices and digital literacy. The conflict between the traditionally protected rights of creators and distributors and the new literacy requires a thoughtful reevaluation of the rights of authors (*droits d'auteur*) and the rights of the public that is part and parcel of the digital environment. It is obviously not feasible, over the long term, to maintain and extend the print culture model of protections, without much adaptation or modification, to the digital realm. Such a situation will lead to either a generalization of a new digital divide, one in which the majority of users will become de facto circumventers of excessively restrictive rules and laws, or to efforts that will amount to imposing legal obstacles (in the name of rights protections) that have the potential to stifle progress and innovation and the development and spread of new technologies. Ultimately, and despite the initial difference between code (or, for simplicity reasons, software) and other creations, the general tendency is the adoption of the Free and Open model of publishing, exchange, and distribution, a model that collapses the differences between code and other artifacts.

VI. Open Access and the Economics of Knowledge

Ultimately, Creative Commons, by making materials available though the popular adoption of its licenses and their digital integration, creates a digital public domain, one that democratizes the production, publication, and distribution of digital objects. Its appeal lies in the fact that it is initially nonspecialist: it does not suffer from the burden of disciplinary customs or weighty traditions. Instead, it benefits from a clear and accessible abstraction of the basic elements of control and publication of any object, and therefore can attract a variety of users. Furthermore, its recent translation into foreign languages, translations that do not merely make its licenses available in other languages but instead generate licenses that are in tune with national copyright and intellectual property laws, have made it a significant player on a global scale.[36] This international dimension has also led to the extension of Creative Commons to other areas, especially to the launch of Science Commons.

Science Commons, described as "devoted to easing unnecessary barriers to the flow of scientific knowledge and technical information,"[37] aims to transfer the Creative Commons model into the arena of scientific research, but it also seeks to address some of the issues raised by the Open Access movement.[38] The founding text of Open Access is the Budapest Open Access Initiative, which focuses on the definition of the conditions that have led to the need for Open Access (namely, the digital environment and the ways in which it has modified the status of information and knowledge) and on specifying what kind of literature is to be made available through Open Access and through what means.[39] The first important aspect of the Initiative is its focus on the learned literature, especially in the sciences and the social sciences. Second, its definition of "open access" highlights the economic dimension of the issue by pointing out the need to overcome price barriers (cost of subscriptions to scientific and specialized journals or the inability of less developed countries to purchase scientific publications, for instance). In other words, the guiding motivation behind Open Access is the free circulation and free access to newly created knowledge. Thus, the definition of Open Access is as follows:

> By "open access" to this literature, we mean its free availability on the public internet, permitting any users to read, download, copy, distribute, print, search, or link to the full texts of these articles, crawl them for indexing, pass them as data to software, or use them for any other lawful purpose, without financial, legal, or technical barriers other than those inseparable from gaining access to the internet itself. The only constraint on reproduction and distribution, and the only role for copyright in this domain, should be to give authors control over the integrity of their work and the right to be properly acknowledged and cited.[40]

Open Access is tied to the digital environment: it is linked to it as the site for the new publication and exchange of knowledge and information. Such a broad definition is, it goes without saying, disturbing, certainly for the traditional publishers of learned and scientific journals and to academic presses, not to mention publishing houses in general. Ultimately, and without focusing on the immediate economic implications of Open Access, the movement adopts and generalizes characteristics we have identified as constitutive of digital literacy as a rationale for radically modifying the scientific and professional publishing landscape. The shift toward almost exclusively digital publications, especially in some scientific fields, requires more than just a transfer of the model of review and evaluation of content: it also needs tools and knowledge necessary for the generation of digitally compatible objects, their distribution, storage, and archival preservation. In other words, it inaugurates a transition to a more coherent digital archives that incorporate into their design and deployment the growing collapse of author and reader functions,[41] as much as the bypassing of traditional editorial functions, especially in scientific publications.[42] The implications of the adoption of Open Access are momentous and numerous (and they have been met with strong resistance from publishers) and go well beyond the difficulties of a financially viable transition from the current situation into a more open and digitally accessible archive. For what they fundamentally modify are the methods with which disciplines have conventionally evaluated themselves: their selection mechanisms, their standards for measuring success and influence, and ultimately importance and significance. Furthermore, by transitioning to a digital Open Access model, expert know-how and work traditionally of limited access or availability will be within reach to almost any online user. While the initial Budapest text seems to center on scientific material, the Berlin statement takes a broader perspective, calling for the generalization of the model to all cultural products and thus explicitly including in its text the Human Sciences. It in fact asks cultural institutions to make their collections available online. It also explicitly articulates some of the implications of the initial Budapest statement, namely, the need to take into account online publications when considering the appointment, promotion, and evaluation of scholarly works.[43]

It is interesting to note that the scientific disciplines, despite some of the current debates about Open Access and its role, have in large part adapted to the new digital environment. Most publications are available in preprint form online and there is little if any distinction between online and in-print status of publication. In the humanities, however, the situation could not be more different. A recent report from the American Council of Learned Societies tried to address this gap and to recommend some solutions that are specific to the humanities and parts of the social sciences.[44] While the report recognizes the need (and in some cases, urgent need) to encourage digital scholarship in the humanities, it remains somewhat timid about what needs to be done in order to move the field into the digital age. It still calls on the established academic hierarchy (the appeal to senior scholars to dabble in digital projects or the emphasis on digitization projects and not on the new models of scholarship made possible by digital technology and literacy, etc.) to manage the slow adaptation to a technology that has already fundamentally changed the knowledge landscape. It is true that the humanities as a discipline are by nature conservative, based on tradition and slow penetration of new paradigms, but in this instance it is somewhat surprising to find a field that has thought a great deal about print, its culture and material support, and their implications for political and social change, at a loss in the face of a similarly pervasive digital technology.[45] Whereas the sciences are forging ahead with their transition, dictating, along the way, the shape and the concentration of the digital libraries of the future, the humanities are something of a baffled spectator seeking guidance from their past and historical ties to print archives and their exploitation.

Literacy, especially digital literacy, as we have seen, is an activity that creates a culture: it is an engagement with objects and their production and symbolic manipulations that puts into place deep structures, from laws to hierarchical social categories. If the culture of the book, with its specific valuation of reading and interpretation, led not only to the institution of the author, but also of professional readers, to what will digital literacy give rise? Who will the *Homo academicus* of the digital environment be? What is ultimately changing, thanks to digital literacy and its pressure to adapt Open Access as the basic model for the circulation of information in the digital environment, is the economy of knowledge itself: how it is valued, the ways it is produced, and the manner in which it can be transferred and reused. In other words, digital literacy, much like the vulgar languages in the late Middle Ages and the early Modern period in Europe, is creating new public and civic spaces; it is inventing a new public sphere and with it a new public altogether. This new public sphere, at the same time both global and local, at the same time both universal and particular, is a challenge not only to jurisdictions but also to most established mechanisms designed to manage property and to protect ownership. In this respect, Open Access (and we will discuss its implication for archiving in our last chapter) is the natural expression of the essential norms of digital literacy.

Perhaps at this juncture we should briefly discuss a success story of Open Access, one that engages directly with digital literacy. I mean the MIT OpenCourseware project.[46] In its own terms it is a "large-scale, Web-based electronic publishing initiative [whose] goals are to: Provide free, searchable access to MIT's course materials for educators, students, and self-learners around the world, [and to] Extend the reach and impact of MIT OCW and the 'opencourseware' concept."[47] The project's success is remarkable, and the more so since it is the first large-scale institutional

Open Access digital learning environment. In this sense, it provides the
first instance of the viability and legitimacy of the Open Access and FOSS
models for top-rank institutions. With projects like OpenCourseWare,
the global economy of knowledge is changed. In this new world of digital
pedagogy and scholarship, access becomes synonymous with literacy, and
users who otherwise would never have had the opportunity to experience
and learn from an institution like MIT become part of its global reach.
But perhaps most importantly, MIT's example will encourage other institutions to liberalize access to their material and to adopt a similar Open
Access scheme. While MIT is a private institution, we can expect public
institutions of higher learning and research to move more easily toward
the adoption of such plans.

Despite its success and its importance, MIT's offering remains relatively static in the sense that it makes available online mostly textual material (syllabi, lecture notes and assignments, bibliographies, etc.). Others
have opted to make available online recorded lectures as podcasts, via
their own Web sites or via Apple's iTunes Store for free. Others have incorporated the iTunes model itself (a store designed to sell digital music)
for managing undergraduate life.[48] In this case, the digital music store
provides the model for organizing and managing life on campus. Students
were given iPods with which they could access Duke University's special
version of iTunes. "Duke on iTunes U is a repository for a variety of multimedia materials related to the Duke educational experience. Students
and instructors in Fall 2006 iPod courses will be participating in the next
phase of our pilot program to explore the use of iTunes U in the academic
context. Participants in this pilot will be able to access digital course materials prepared by the instructor, exchange digital audio and video files, set
up course podcasts, and synchronize multimedia content to their iPods
quickly and easily."[49] Duke's iTunes U is perhaps the first experiment with
the educational potential of digital literacy. It draws on the latest tools and
expects students to be sufficiently literate to take full advantage of the
digital offerings. It tries to simulate the digitization, under the currently
available technology, of some important components of the learning experience. In this respect it merges the real with the virtual and allows for
experimentation in the fluid nature of the digital environment and the
ways in which it relates, but it also shapes perceptions and actions in the

material world. It offers a new metaphor for schooling, a metaphor derived from a digital model that itself is based on a history of digital technology and the evolution of interfaces. In other words, it signals a recognition of the potential for the use of digital literacy in order to improve and modernize learning environments. The hybrid nature of the program is essential because it permits students and teachers to evaluate the dynamic interplay between the two environments and to exploit new opportunities for collaboration. The synergy provided by the flexibility of the model and the ubiquitous nature of the technologies used offer promising opportunities for exchanging knowledge outside of the initial boundaries of Duke and its managed network. By encouraging the creation of digital objects by all participants to record their reactions to the experiment, it also invites newer and at times unexpected transmission of knowledge.

Ultimately, such projects pave the way for the full realization of digital literacy in increasingly networked environments. They also demonstrate the emergence of new learned and learning environments that are neither utopian nor unrealistic. To the contrary, they rely on available technology. They also feature the distributed and collaborative (and anthological) digital environment as a point of departure and also extend the models of openness and freedom of access and exchange to newer contexts. What is perhaps most intriguing about such experiments is the fact that they allow all participants to function in a world where access and distribution are natural, where there are no obstacles to the manipulation and transformation of information and objects. Indeed, such is the purpose of learning, and at least in cases such as these, it would seem that the Free and Open model is more suited and more adapted to the emerging digital environment for learning.

We began our survey of Free and Open Access with a religious guiding metaphor, one that opposes heresy and orthodoxy. With the advancement of digital technologies and the rise of digital practices, the heretical model, one of Free and Open Access to the digital objects in their diversity and density and one that is cognizant of their susceptibility to conversions, is emerging as the dominant framework for digital practices. Heresy as dissidence has transformed the digital landscape itself into the land of dissidence, dissidence against the weight of restrictive notions of freedom, dissidence against the continued imposition of inappropriate conventions governing the public domain, and dissidence against unfair interpretations of normal and customary digital practices. Attitudes toward code, the material and discursive production of software, have come to shape expectations about digital objects and to inform the rules of comportment, with their financial and political implications, in the digital environment. This trend is best embodied by the emergence of what we called Web OS, or the shift from the complete reliance on desktop resident operating systems and storage to manage one's presence and work online to a more distributed, shared, and freely accessible network version. But along with this shift and the freedoms it offers come risks and dangers that affect not only identity (privacy and security) but also fundamental conceptions about the ownership of data produced by users and hosted by providers. Who owns what and what are the relations between those who author and exchange information and those who host them and transmit their communications? How are the currently responsible parties to negotiate the migration from print archives to digital ones; how are they to manage the selection of what is to be digitized, in what format, by whom; and how will they determine under what access rules to make it available? It is highly significant that Google has recently announced that it is joining the Open Source Open Invention Network, a patent-sharing community that aims at providing support for Linux and related Open Source projects. Considering Google's status and its treasure chest of in-house development, the long-term intellectual and economic potentials are most promising for the Open Source community and ecosystem.[50] These are but a few of the questions that the new economy of digital knowledge makes urgent.

The transition to digital archives, along with the questions of access and of integrity and security, raises essentially ethical and political concerns. Perhaps Pascal framed the question best when he wondered about the authorities that control access to truth and morality: "This with paintings seen from afar or from near. And there is only but one indivisible point which is the true one, all others are either too close or too distant, too high or too low. Perspective assigns this point in art. But in matters of truth and morality who will assign it?"[51] He who owns and controls the archive will control a significant part of the future, our digital future. Authority, it would seem, comes with not only the tools but also the archive itself, and therefore it is relevant to ask who is archiving digital history, for what purposes, and according to which rules? What about our recent digital past? Has it been recorded, preserved, and by whom? It is as if we are in the Wild West with a first-come-first-served attitude. But once the digital environment has become the main interface for our social, economic, and political actions, the archive will take on an increasingly important role. And, if indeed digital identity, while polyphonic, is nevertheless based on aggregation, then the archive, the digital archive of the recent past and our continuing interactions with it, will hold the secrets for its future exploitation and perhaps abuse. Because of the history of the digital environment, the archive has become the de facto property of private entities due to the openness (and we forget the search engines' indexing of publicly available Web sites was perhaps the first large-scale case of Open Access); it is fair to ask questions about its ownership, its management, and its uses and potential abuses? For with increasing openness and the growing reliance on Web-hosted services, individual transactions become more valuable because they provide the tools for the construction of digital identity. Our digital future is shaped in large part by our current actions online. Our digital past, however, is not necessarily preserved, nor is it necessarily available.

4

Archiving the Future

Two recent anecdotes are perhaps the best introduction to the subject of our concluding chapter. They both illustrate the fragility of digital archives and the continuing difficulty in transitioning into a digital archive for some major industries.

First, an Associated Press story about a technician's error led to the permanent erasure of 800,000 electronic images that contained records in Alaska's Permanent Fund:

> Perhaps you've experienced that sinking feeling when a single keystroke accidentally destroys hours of work. Now imagine wiping out a disk drive containing an account worth $38 billion.
>
> That's what happened to a computer technician reformatting a disk drive at the Alaska Department of Revenue. While doing routine maintenance work, the technician accidentally deleted applicant information for an oil-funded account—one of Alaska residents' biggest perks—and mistakenly reformatted the backup drive, as well.

There was still hope, until the department discovered its third line of defense had failed: backup tapes were unreadable.

"Nobody panicked, but we instantly went into planning for the worst-case scenario," said Permanent Fund Dividend Division Director Amy Skow. The computer foul-up last July would end up costing the department more than $200,000.

Over the next few days, as the department, the division and consultants from Microsoft Corp. and Dell Inc. labored to retrieve the data, it became obvious the worst-case scenario was at hand.

Nine months worth of information concerning the yearly payout from the Alaska Permanent Fund was gone: some 800,000 electronic images that had been painstakingly scanned into the system months earlier, the 2006 paper applications that people had either mailed in or filed over the counter, and supporting documentation such as birth certificates and proof of residence. And the only backup was the paperwork itself—stored in more than 300 cardboard boxes.[1]

In this case, three details stand out: (1) the ease with which errors can become catastrophic in the digital environment; (2) not only the failure of hardware and equipment, but the fact that a backup existed but was unreadable; and (3) the value of old-fashioned original material needed to reconstruct what was lost. A tape was still available, but because of format and systems changes, it had simply become obsolete. It is an archive with a dead interface, or without any available interface. In other words, digital archiving needs to take into account not only the existence of digital objects, but their accessibility and the cost of redigitizing from the original paper documents. But what about cases where there are no longer paper archives? What about archives where the only record is digital?

Second, consider a recent article in *Variety* about Hollywood's encounter with digital archiving. The problem discussed here is symptomatic not only of the entertainment industry's dilemma but of cultural institutions, governments, and similar entities who require large-scale storage and archiving of reusable multimedia material. Here are the basics of the story:

As far as movies are concerned, digital, like diamonds, was supposed to be forever. No more dyes to fade, no more film stocks to decay or catch fire. Just pristine digital data, preserved for all time, and release prints as clear and sharp as the images caught by the camera.

Just one problem: For long-term storage, digital is—so far—proving to be a time bomb, more permanent than sand painting but not much else. Simply put, there's no generally accepted way to store digital "footage" for more than a few months. After that the industry is using a hodgepodge of improvised solutions, some rather costly, others not very reliable.

That looked like a small problem when digital filmmaking was limited to low-budget indies, animation houses and tech pioneers like James Cameron and George Lucas. Now, though, that small problem is growing geometrically as the major studios shift away from film to digital capture. Such recent releases as "300," "Apocalypto," "Zodiac" and "Superman Returns" were shot on digital. Their digital masters could be seriously degraded if the problem isn't addressed quickly.

In fact, the problem is so severe that the Academy of Motion Picture Arts & Sciences' and Technology Council warned in 2005 that within just a few years films shot with digital cameras could be lost. It's not that there's no way to store digital data. On the contrary, there are dozens of ways to store it, most of which go obsolete in just a few years. Remember 5″ floppies and Zip disks? And the disks that have stuck around? Not so reliable . . .

Data tapes are balky and can fall apart. Data DVDs and CDs have a history of "rotting" and can't be counted on to last as long as their commercially pressed cousins. Plus there's no reason to expect that the computers of 20 years from now—never mind 100—will be able to plug in to today's hard disks.[2]

In this case, we face the ephemeral nature of digital formats and the incompatibility of systems and the general problem of interoperability. The solution, at least for the time being, seems to rely on a reverse conversion, a return to the old-fashioned film while waiting for a technological answer that most experts agree will never be fully satisfactory. What is important in this case is that neither cost nor storage is a factor. Instead, it is the technology or the *digitality* itself that appears to be the source of the problem, even in cases where film was digitally captured.

Any individual user who has had to migrate from one computer to another is undoubtedly aware of the difficulties involved in preserving data and moving it between systems. Changing applications and formats—the exponential growth of data collected and saved by users and institutions alike; the spread of personal data between desktop machines and online hosted services, not to mention the rapid rate of transition to newer storage media that render previous ones obsoletes—are all but an indication of the current muddied state of digital archiving. In fact, we can safely say that one of the most often neglected or forgotten aspects of digital culture is, ultimately, the impermanence or fragility of information and its material support. Users behave as if digital information will always be the same, always accessible, and always searchable. And yet, a quick look into the brief history of digital culture demonstrates the futility of such a point of view. Most have a utopian belief in the mysterious powers of technology to convert and preserve their essential information, despite their experience. It is as if the ease of use and the facility with which we can initiate new accounts online and adopt new systems and formats amounts to a surreptitious but natural conversion of our digital past. But digital history is literally littered with the remains of old and forgotten formats and media and with the ruins of inaccessible machines and systems.

Furthermore, with the growing engagement with the digital environment, we are producing more data, storing more material, exchanging more e-mails, and ultimately we are becoming data consumers. The rise of this data-consumption culture has contributed to a diversification of the data we produce and collect and has increased the amount of data collected about us. To some degree, this is one of the defining characteristics of the digital environment: every transaction, every search request or Web site visit, everything related to online presence can be tracked, recorded, and stored and ultimately searched and mined. While this dimension of online activity points to privacy and security issues, it also invites us to think about who is collecting the data about our digital habits, for what purposes. It also incites us to look with more care into the laws that currently govern such data collection and their potential uses. What should be the role of governments in requiring data- retention laws and in protecting the privacy of citizens against abusive exploitation of collected data? Such data has become remarkably rich and diverse: it covers not only information stored by ISPs, Web sites, and eCommerce providers, but also mobile phone services, search engines, and governments. It has also become the site of production of new categories: new categories of behavior and new categories of digital objects that, because of their nature, require unique abstractions in order to archive and preserve them. The digital archive, much like digital culture itself, while it shares some basic and essential characteristics with print culture, also has new and challenging features that call for a thoughtful evaluation of our archival politics and strategies, at the individual level as well as at the institutional and national levels. If anything characterizes the early history of digital culture in the twentieth century, it is the poverty of its archive. It is ironic that a culture that is firmly grounded in the automation of recording and tracking every action in its environment lacks a comprehensive and reliable archive of its own. Such forgetting is neither innocent nor to be summarily dismissed as a mere accident of history: it points to a serious cultural and, ultimately, economic and political blindness. The early record of digital culture is distinguished by its gaps and omissions. It is the victim of its own early success and rapid adoption. Whereas print culture gave rise to a histori-cally reliable archive (that, in relative terms, required little intervention), digital culture, based in change and continuous conversions, has produced at best a fragmented archive. A change such as this can be momentous be-cause, over the long term, it has the potential to alter our historical per-spective and to inform the ways in which we define and understand the notion of a record, of historical record, and the narratives we will be able to produce about the events that determine our cultural history. The dy-namic nature of digital culture has not so far given rise to a new dynamic of historical recording of the actions and objects that are the material of digital literacy.

The problem of digital archives is obviously not limited to the difficul-ties in preserving and transmitting the recent and current state of the digital environment. It also concerns the obstacles facing nations and gov-ernments in designing affordable and feasible conversions of traditional archives into digital formats. The problems here are numerous, and they range from the selection of material to be digitized to the process of digi-tization itself. They also relate to devising platforms and mechanisms for making such archives accessible while maintaining their integrity and security. Furthermore, they force us to think about the status of the converted or digitized object: Is it simply a copy (especially when it can be available in multiple versions and formats) or a legal equivalent of the original? Can it reproduce all the features of the original or are we to settle for an acceptable reproduction? Printed books can exist in multiple editions and multiple versions: digital versions tend to eliminate such differences by converting the old into the new without necessarily preserving any traces of their differences. While digital technology is powerful enough to reproduce an image of texts, for example, it cannot yet reproduce texture. So, for the time being, it would seem that we will have a hybrid archival universe, one in which print and digital coexist, but in which access to the digital will increase while access to the print will become the domain of the few and the privileged. But my main point here is simply to point out the potential implications of the emergence of digital archiving and some of its inherent shortcomings. Will it be possible to have digital archives equivalent to our current historical records and archives? Is such an archive at all desirable, or should we assume that with the rise of digital culture and its literacy we should expect new forms of archives to become relevant, and ones that do not necessarily correspond to our long reliance on print and its predecessors become irrelevant?

Digital archives have, if our recent history holds any truth, a limited life of usability because of the continually changing standards, file formats, and protocols. Therefore, they will always require not only preservation in the traditional sense of the term, but digital preservation: that is to say, conversion into newer and emerging and hopefully more reliable formats. Thus, interoperability and compatibility are basic features of any design of a framework for digital archiving and this requirement becomes a strong argument for the need for open formats. While currently debates rage about Open Formats between private companies and Open Source groups and governments, I think it is essential to keep in mind the historical need for Open Formats that cover not only documents but also an array of other important digital manipulations that range from compression (used to reduce storage space) to encryption (used sometimes to secure files or archives), to database formats. The conversion into a digital archive, while holding tremendous potential, also comes with its own set of problems and obstacles. We are no longer naïve enough to believe in the promise that new technologies will always manage to improve and simplify if not resolve past problems. If anything, digital technology has proven that it evolves by forgetting or even at times ignoring its own recent past: it advances by abandoning what did not either work or succeed. Such a norm may be useful in reducing the glut of information produced, but it does not succeed in maintaining and preserving information we need or want to preserve.

These introductory remarks are meant to highlight the need to think about the value of digital archiving and the values that digital archives incarnate or generate. We can already see some of these trends emerge, from various quantitative analyses of network-specific structure to the Long Tail effect, to name only the most obvious.[3] But for the most part, it is safe to say at this point in time that overall, quantitative aspects of digital culture have been dominant for understandable reasons with some small but significant efforts to study the emerging social networks and their ecosystems.

I. Web Histories: Between the Archive and the Index

The first archives of the digital environment were search indexes. Search engines were the first automated tools to take advantage of the open nature of the network, visiting publicly available Web sites, indexing them, and ultimately storing snapshots of their changes and evolutions. Thus it is not surprising to find that currently the two most comprehensive archives of the Internet as we know it belong to search companies. First, there is the Wayback Machine and its Internet Archive.[4] The Wayback Machine performs a remarkable public service by making available its archives. It has collected snapshots of Web sites since 1996, and its archives are easily searchable, making it possible to study or follow the evolution of a particular Web site or to observe the effects of new technologies or emerging trends on the design and functionality of sites. But because it is essentially a well-behaved search index, it respects the Robots.txt and thus allows sites to specify whether they are willing to be indexed and included in the archive or whether they opt to be excluded.[5] Between the choice of sites and the gaps within the archive itself, we have a valuable but at best fragmentary record of the Internet since 1996. And because the tool used to visit sites is essentially a search robot, the results vary significantly, from parsing a full document to indexing Metatags or simply the first paragraphs of HTML pages. In other words, we may have a reliable record of only some parts of the indexed Web sites, and the selection can vary according to the design and method of each robot.

At the same time, the Wayback Machine makes the writing of some histories of the Internet and its evolution possible, although it is also equally plausible to write a history of the exclusions and gaps in the archive. In other words, and especially since we can see what is missing from the archive, we can speculate as to the reasons for such absences or omissions and interpret them accordingly. In any case, we have with the Wayback Machine an initial tool for *an* archive (unfortunately, and despite its value, it seems to be the only accessible one) of the early history of the digital environment, an archive that tells us as much about the culture of the Net as it does about the obstacles and difficulties of creating and maintaining its archive. From a historical point of view, this is rather remarkable since for most of us we are describing here events and objects that we either participated in creating or witnessed, but without a full record of the experience. The collective memory of the Internet and its culture has a formidable number of blank pages in it.[6] The archive, however, is in the public domain and as such it plays an important role in making a snapshot of digital history accessible to all. Furthermore, its Open Access illustrates, and this despite the partial nature of the archive, the evolution of digital literacy and its intertwining with technologies and practices from the early textual Web to the current multimedia hubs. We can also retrace the shift from static homepages, as relatively stable entry points into personal and collective Web sites, into the current model driven by RSS and similar subscribe-and-deliver paradigms. These changes are revealing because they demonstrate how practices and technologies converge to form values and expectations, creating along the way new economic models and forums for digital sociability. A cultural history of the digital environment remains to be written and archives like the ones maintained by the Wayback Machine will feature prominently in such an effort.

The second archive, also the result of search indexing, is the one owned and maintained by Google. It seems to fair to assume that Google has over time built a parallel archive of the Internet in its server farms. While the presence of such an archive is extremely valuable and raises legitimate concerns about its ownership, Google has recently begun to exploit it in a number of promising ways. In this case, we see once again the development of an archival strategy firmly based on the requirements for efficient searching. Accuracy, speed, relevance, and reliability are essential for successful search engines, and they are also essential for an archive. Google recently introduced its Web History service to users with a Google account.[7] The service requires users to allow Google to keep track of their browsing, but it also offers them a rich and detailed history of their searches and their navigation and tools to organize, visualize, and analyze their recorded online presence by Google. In effect, Google's Web History is a historical Index, an aggregate of transactions created by combining search queries and visited Web sites that can produce a personal historical narrative for the digital identity associated with the Google account in question. In this model, the archive is no longer passive nor is it a simple repository of information or a record of past interests. Instead, it is activated through its dynamic association with current navigation and searching; it is the site of digital memory, or the memorial site for a digital identity's memory. As such, Web History provides different snapshots of digital existence: it allows for the reconstruction of microcosmic interests and the analysis of their relations to either personal history or to broader trends and events. It is certainly a more powerful and more revealing tool that focuses on the digital events initiated by an identity (and users may have multiple Google identities) that will give us insight into the mechanics of digital identity as it unfolds on the network and through the perspective of *searchability* and *findability*. Obviously, within such an environment, patterns emerge to reflect either personal choices or concerns and shifts in pattern signal changing perspectives. With such a tool, we can imagine digital biographies of roaming digital identities discovering the hidden treasures of the digital environment or simply following a trail of adventure and discovery. In a short period of time, it is likely that the History tool will become the site of an open version of Second Life,[8] one in which users have the luxury of managing their preferences and editing what is to be used in the construction of their Web Histories. While Second Life mimics the real world in a virtual environment, Web History is digital through and through: it takes the polyphonic dimension of digital identity and allows it to manage its own representations.

The Wayback Machine and Google's Web History are two tools that emerged from searching and that resulted in the archiving of extensive digital data about the digital environment and its participants. They both negotiate with the digital transposition of temporality through its digital expression and promise us access to an emerging historicity of the digital environment that is neither grounded in the absoluteness of the past nor in the privileges of the present. Instead, each in its own way devises mechanisms for the digital conversion of history, for the productions of historical voices native to the digital environment. If the Wayback Machine is marked by gaps and absences, Google's Web History is characterized by an assumed completeness. As long as the user is logged into his account, the system records and tracks his queries and associated actions. While trends easily emerge, what remains mysterious are the intentions or motivations behind them, although, from the digital perspective, such a lack is not necessarily an issue or a concern. The Index, this absolute condensation of the content of the digital environment, receives in this case a personalized expression: it is individualized and reduced to represent a reflection of multiple trajectories. In short, Web History shows the potential of the digital archive in giving rise to potentially self-reflective digital tools.

The problem, of course, is the ownership of this archive and its control. Google, while allowing users to control what to be retained in their profiles, nevertheless maintains full control over the entirety of the archive and can choose to deploy its content or its analysis in any way it chooses. Google's Archive and its associated Index are the property of the company, along with the records of their usage. It would seem that at this point Google holds some of the most valuable collective and individual memories of the digital environment. And with the introduction of desktop tools from Google (as well as other companies), this archive now can transparently accumulate records of digital activity and interest that combine local and network-based activities. The phenomenal growth of Google testifies to the attraction of its model and to the relevance of the archive as a principle for an organizing presence in the digital environment. From Gmail to Google's Office Suite, the initial promise has always been fast and accurate searching on hosted content as well as free storage. In other words, the promise of Google is the promise of the digital archive itself, of the archive that is created by users and their actions, of the archive that is the product of the spread of digital literacy. Thus it is not surprising to find Google seeking to expand its founding model to encompass the traditional archive, the one normally hosted by libraries and represented by printed books and print archival material.

II. The World's Card Catalogue, or the Anthological Index?

Google's Book Search[9] has generated so much controversy that it has become difficult to recall precisely what the original project or its actual implementation was. Its reception, especially by publishers, some national libraries, and Google's rivals, has eclipsed the significance of such a large-scale digitization of printed books. My concern in the remarks that follow is largely focused on the status of the project as an extension of Google's overall model of the Index and the Archive (Google explicitly describes its project as in part a digital extension of the traditional library catalogue),[10] and on the issues it raises concerning the ownership and controls of archival material and its digital distribution and accessibility. Before examining public efforts to design frameworks for national-scale archives and their affiliations with projects for digital patrimony, it is instructive to look into the workings of the project because it affords us insight into the curatorship and preservation of digitized material and the changing roles of libraries and librarians.

The Google Book Search combines the digitization of books with their indexing: it makes digital versions of books available and searchable online, merging their index with Google's general Index. Furthermore, it presents the books in different ways according to their copyright status: if they are in the public domain, they are readable online and are also available for downloading in PDF format. If they are under copyright protection, Google presents the reader with a full bibliographic description of the book and with access to a limited number of pages (these can vary according to the copyright holders' wishes). Such a scheme has the advantage of making accessible online out-of-print and public domain books while at the same time increasing access to more recent publications. In a sense, it consists of a coherent Google strategy that centers on the archive's Index as the core attraction. In this case, it is only a natural extension to increase the already available Index by adding to it records and in some instances full access to indexed items, and eventually to make the content available via the growing Google services. For ultimately, the great difference between Google's offering and others is precisely searching and its reliability. As an example, the BNF digitization project and its Gallica[11] undertaking demonstrates the importance of searchability (and in this light, the new release of an early version of the French portion of Europeana shows how difficult it is to deliver fully searchable digitized books). Most publishers are also not well-prepared for the task. So it would seem that collaborative projects between IT companies and publishers are the solution and the way to provide competitors to Google Book Search.

So far, the critiques of Book Search have largely concentrated on two dimensions: possible copyright infringement and the fear of a Google monopoly over the digital culture of the book. For copyright infringement, it remains to be seen how the courts will decide on the issue and how they will evaluate the validity of fair use claimed by Google. But along with the potential infringement, most publishers and some IT companies have articulated arguments concerning the proper or acceptable ways to manage the transition to the digital archives while respecting the "creative process" and intellectual property. In this view, by choosing to adopt an opt-out model, Google is simply "taking" works and digitizing them without full consultation with publishers and especially without fully protecting the rights of copyright holders and creators. This view was most clearly expressed by Thomas C. Rubin, Microsoft's Associate General Council for Copyright, in a speech delivered during the March 2007 Association of American Publishers meeting:[12]

So the question we need to ask ourselves is: What path will we as a society choose in making the world's books and publications available online? Will we choose a path that nourishes creativity and innovation over the long term and that preserves incentives for authors to offer their best works online? Or will we choose a path that encourages companies simply to "take" the works of others, without any regard for copyright or the impact of their actions on authors and publishers too?

This technology [Turning the Page, developed jointly by Microsoft and The British Library],[13] which the British Library intends to use only on texts that are no longer under copyright, is making it possible for people around the world to directly experience some of the world's rarest and most treasured books that form the basis of our history and our culture.

Google's chosen path would no doubt allow it to make more books searchable online more quickly and more cheaply than others, and in the short term this will benefit Google and its users. But the question is, at what long-term cost? In my view, Google has chosen the wrong path for the longer term, because it systematically violates copyright and deprives authors and publishers of an important avenue for monetizing their works. In doing so, it undermines critical incentives to create. This violates the second principle I mentioned. Google has also undertaken this path without any attempt to reach an agreement with affected publishers and authors before engaging in copying. This violates both the second and third principles.[14]

Rubin's remarks articulate the position of many in the publishing business in the United States and Europe. A second component of the argument states basically that the scale and scope of Book Search will result in a Google monopoly, a feeling that is also shared by many, especially by those who are sensitive to the cultural differences and the need to take into account diverse customs and traditions while digitally constructing an archive that is fundamentally a cultural archive and a digital construct of cultural identity and history. And finally, a third dimension addresses the technological efforts to create a functional and workable digital reading experience. Thus, in this critique three fundamental issues are emerging: the role to be played by current copyright and intellectual property laws in shaping the structure of the emerging digital archive; the role to be played by current actors in the publishing field and the cultural heritage sector in avoiding the creation of a monopoly that can also become not only a monopoly of access but also a monoculture of interfaces and models for the digital life of digitized cultural artifacts; and finally, the efforts to develop technologies aimed at making the digital environment a reading environment for objects like books.

But Microsoft and U.S. publishers are not alone in declining to go along with Google's Book Search. We find a different criticism in the recent *République 2.0* report drafted by Michel Rocard. It is worth citing at length because it articulates clearly the cultural and political dimension of the debate in terms that associate cultural identity with the design and implementation of the digital archive. In this case, we have the opposition between Google's unspecified but assumed American model and the plea for a European alternative:

> Few of the French accept the cultural dominance of the United States, and most Europeans will probably support the European digital library project, which is a worthy response to Google Book Search. This is why Europeana, as it is called, merits our wholehearted support.
>
> The only effective answer to Google has to be European. Yet the European search engine Quaero is in trouble since the withdrawal of its German component. The European satellite navigation system Galileo has yet to be launched even though the majority of European cars are already equipped with GPS. It is important that the European digital library project not suffer the same fate, yet at this moment in time, only Hungary and Portugal have joined the French project. If not the sign of complete failure, this nonetheless suggests the current impotence of our "European" digital library.
>
> Europeana needs to be more than just a good idea, thoroughly French, idealistic and finally unrealistic because not based on a viable model. Rather than confronting Google, then, merely with public political stances, perhaps the French minister of culture ought to have thought through first the structure of his alliance with his other potential partners in their competition with Google Book Search. That way, the National Library of France would not have had to go it alone. Perhaps he should have negotiated a truly European project in advance, rather than dooming France to be the sole motivating force. We cannot allow Google to maintain a monopoly on the digitizing of our memory and our history. It is crucial to keep in mind as well all of the issues concerning interoperability, the problems of the

Internet and its forms of free access and individual liberty that Google may be the only group to manage if they alone digitize the world's printed patrimony.[15]

It would seem that the solution proposed or at least suggested by Michel Rocard calls for, first, the expansion of the Europeana project in order to make it fully European; and second, the alliance with other private IT companies in order to counter the weight and the dominance of Google and the scale of its undertaking. But, at this time at least, the only realistic possible ally is Microsoft, and unfortunately such an alliance (as demonstrated in numerous projects, and in Turning the Page as well) would also contradict the last remark of the citation above. Microsoft seems to be only willing to deliver technologies, interfaces, and tools that rely on its operating system and its browser: it has had a history of exploiting its privileged situation as the provider of the majority of desktop systems and leveraging them to advance its business model. While Google's project, despite its universal aims and potential threats of homogenization, delivers its Archive in an open format and in one that excludes neither an operating system nor a browser; its interface is a Web interface that has become synonymous with interoperability and compatibility with most systems and browsers. Thus, if indeed there is a need to find a balancing to Google's dominance, it will have to take into account the need to deliver access in an open and standard fashion. For the Open Access model in this case means more than just access to the digitized text: it also implies the ability to search, download, print, and manipulate public domain material.

But what are Google's business plans for the Book Search? An article in the London *Times* gives us an insight into what is to come and its potential implications for digitization and its relation to print: "With 380m people using Google each month, the move would give a significant boost to the development of e-books and have a big impact on the publishing industry and book retailers. Jens Redmer, director of Google Book Search in Europe, said: 'We are working on a platform that will let publishers give readers full access to a book online.'"

He did not believe taking books online would mean the end of the printed word but it would give readers more options when it came to buying. "You may just want to rent a travel guide for the holiday or buy a chapter of a book. Ultimately, it will be the readers who decide how books are read," he said.[16] "What emerges here is the Google's plans to extend the digital environment, through its interface to the Index and the Archive, finally to include eBooks. Google's objectives are to be seen and interpreted in this light, and not only from the perspective of possible copyright infringement or abuse of the Fair Use clause or in meddling in the traditional publisher's business model. The massive digitization, coupled with powerful indexing and simple yet effective delivery of digital objects, bear the hallmark of a concerted effort to redefine radically the rather morbid landscape of digital books. In doing so, Google demonstrates the commercial viability of the anthological dimension of digital literacy along rather familiar and by now established models (the iTunes store, with Ad Sense advertisement). While the financial stakes are enormous, what is of concern to us here are the cultural components and implications of such a deployment of the digital archive of digitized books, for it is the activity of reading itself that will be transformed and transfigured. Readers will be able to rent or purchase chapters or sections of books, much like users purchase individual songs from iTunes. In the case of text, however, searching is more powerful and more detailed, and therefore allows for the fragmentation and segmentation of a text into more divisions than merely chapters or sections. Thus, one can imagine a user buying a number of pages or choosing to lease a combination of chapters from a book. (Obviously such schemes will require complex rights management for copyright books.) The benefits for Google are enormous: they increase traffic to its sites, they increase the size and the relevance of its Index, and they transfer, at least for a significant category of books, reading activity into a result of searching and indexing.

In short, such an activity will redefine the digital book in significant ways, and along with it the activity of digital reading itself and the literacy within the digital environment. The digital archive, in this instance at least, becomes the agency of a radical conversion: the conversion of the printed book into a digital object whose primary interface will become searching and the indexing, thus transforming the book itself from a relatively autonomous and coherent construct into a tabular and indexical structure. Here, the searcher/potential reader becomes all powerful: he can compose his own selection from various books and works, literally creating the space for an ultimate personal anthological environment that is reproducible and exchangeable online. The personal anthologies of the early Modern period will have been resurrected through the combination of digital books and their indexing. How will authors and publishers respond to such a potential transformation of the traditional book? Will authors begin writing some books with such a reading in mind? In other words, will they write for the Index and the Archive in its digital incarnation? Obviously not all books lend themselves to easy anthologizing, but it is surprising how such a possibility can reshape the production of reading material. What will literary creation be as a digital practice?

For all search engines, the materiality of the Index is reduced to its iconic interface, informing all access to content and shaping the reception of content. For Google's Book Search, and this is perhaps one of its most radical dimensions, has the potential to erase or at least make most of us forget the difference between the digital and the digitized, between objects that when brought into the digital environment are in effect transformed into something other, and objects whose construct and design take their point of departure and some of their intelligibility from the materiality of print and its culture. It is perhaps in this context that we should think about the often-repeated criticism of Book Search and its impact on the "creative process." In most cases the "creative process" is a euphemism for a conservative defense of copyright and the need to extend current protections into the digital environment with little if any consideration of its specificities. Thus, it is often coupled with calls for Digital Rights Management or controls over access to content that tend to go against some of the basic freedoms embedded within digital culture. But, we can also see that digital literacy, in its expansion and in its digitization of the heritage of print culture and its associated memories and histories, has the potential to give birth to new forms of readings that, while reminiscent of earlier practices, are also likely to produce new forms of creativity at the expense of some of the older ones. The book as an object is not likely to disappear anytime soon, but it is also clear that it is no longer the sole or even the primary object for the production of knowledge and its exchange and transmission. And this transformation is what drives the need and the care required for thinking through the emerging digital archives.

III. Patrimony and the New Digital Objects

Google's Book Search shows the way for a potentially radical modification of the cultural landscape, thanks to the massive digitization and indexing of print archives and its consequences for literacy. But, the digital archives are still in their early stages and few if any have been deployed at a national scale. In fact, in most developed countries, there have been studies of the requirements—technological, political, financial, and cultural—for the creation and deployment of such archives. Numerous ongoing projects exist today, from the United Kingdom to Taiwan.[17] Nations and international organizations alike are recognizing the importance of digital archives and the necessity for thinking through their implementation and financing. For our purposes here, I will mostly discuss the U.S. plans, formulated in a series of reports prepared for the Library of Congress and its Digital Preservation Initiative. These plans are also part of the U.S. national Digital Libraries.[18]

Most studies of future digital archives share in common a set of concerns and issues: the distinction between digital material and material that needs to be digitized and the specificities of each group; the need for an infrastructure that can handle the large-scale deployment of national digital archives, its design and financing; the importance of taking into account digital practices and the unique nature of current and emerging digital objects because they will constitute the core of the archives; the necessity to implement security features in order to preserve the integrity of the archives and to manage rights-protected access to the archives; the need for a design of interfaces appropriate for such digital archives and their expected usage and manipulation by users. The studies all share relatively similar points of departure: the necessity to begin the transition from current archives and curatorial methods into digital ones and the undertaking of consultations meant to develop methodologies and consensus on what is to be selected to be digitized. In other words, we have here national plans for digital patrimony, plans that take into account the current hybrid nature of the patrimony and the heightened perception of the risks as well as the promises of digital culture. The first step toward such digital archives consists in the identification of what has been termed "most historically significant" cultural materials, irrelevant of medium and format.

Then follows the collection, digitization, and organization of the digitized objects in order to make them eventually accessible to the public. The work here, and this can be long and complex, will first have to settle on a broad and representative selection of material that is not exclusive of any group, point of view, or historical period. For it is assumed that with the deployment of digital archives the majority of users will use them instead of their originals, and therefore it is crucial to have a solid and viable selection digitized in order not to radically modify the cultural landscape. Furthermore, the selection process assumes, and it would seem correctly, that not everything can and will be digitized. In other words, it takes into account the continued coexistence of a hybrid archive. The digital dream of the absolute library in which every printed object will be accessible does not appear to be realistic. Instead, we are more likely to have divided libraries and archives, appealing to different interests and concerns but in which, with perhaps the exception of very few, the majority of access and consultation will eventually move into the digital environment, although growing or even excessive digitization will have the result of increasing the "exotic" appeal of the old-fashioned archive.

Print and other nondigital objects selected for inclusion in the emerging digital archives pose a series of difficult obstacles, each pertaining to the nature of the object, its form or design, and its materiality. These range from manuscript and rare books to early photographs and sound recordings. While it is easy to convert them into digital objects, it is not necessarily as easy to have the digitized objects be the equivalent to the original. For example, footnotes are much easier to handle in print than in digital form and digitized objects will have to take that into account when deciding on how to preserve digitally a book with extensive footnotes or a book in which footnotes and their complex structure play an important role.[19] But also, the materiality of print objects presents librarians and curators with fundamental choices: Should they continue, by extension, the current practice of preserving a rare or fragile object, by making available a facsimile copy of it, or should they instead take advantage of digital technology and its tools and associate the digitized objects with additional information, thus shaping access and reception to the object by the choice of added tools and information? The question raises serious issues, since it can, depending on the choices made and their generalization, amount to

an indirect imposition of a politics of reading and of interpreting historical documents and founding texts. There are no innocent or neutral tools,
especially when such tools directly shape and organize the reading experience of texts and images. What is informative in this case is the fact that
the context plays a determining role in forming opinions and ideas, and the
digital environment is a contextual construct based on literacy and digital
practices that can be seductive enough to be adapted without deliberation
as paradigmatic for the presentation of digitized material. Librarians are
aware of this potential of digital technology,[20] but the decision on how to
digitize and what to digitize should not be the sole realm of libraries and librarians. Digital technology transforms the library itself into a new space:
it first makes it, thanks to the networked nature of the digital environment, the site of access not only to the local collections but also to other
online collections; second, it redefines the curatorial mission of the library; third, it changes the nature of the index or the library catalog by
introducing a different kind of searchability into the process. For instance,
the organization of the catalog by title, by subject, or by author, essential
to the long history of the library and its hosting of knowledge categories
and their cultural representations and preservation, has to adapt to the
digital index and its conceptualization of the object and its abstractions of
its content.

Finding books in the library is facilitated by the imposed representa-
tional structure and its abstractions of knowledge production. Finding information online is equally governed by abstractions and representations,
but they are different. They are currently generated from a combined effort, joining the parsing of content with metadata that gives a digital representation about an object, its authorship, its subject matter, its place of
publication, and so on. While such data about data is essential and will play
an increasingly important role in the automated and self-discovery systems, naming conventions and standards will become crucial if we are to
have an interoperable digital archive. Furthermore, the identification of
digital objects by unique and permanent markers (such as the DOI)[21] will
alleviate some of the difficulties of finding digitized objects. Metadata is
both, in the case of digital archives, a standard way for marking and identifying objects, and a set of management tools that allows collections to be
separated from access tools and their interfaces. In other words, metadata

will function as a bridge between automated systems and their interfaces to the archive and its catalogs as well as between users and the tools that will allow them to search, identify, and access objects. Some implementations already showcase sophisticated and promising uses of the technology in scientific digital archives. A researcher can generate an RSS subscription that will inform him of any new publications tagged with the chosen topics of interest, and linking the new object to the related ones already available in the archive or identified by the researcher. Tools such as these, combining technologies from various components of the digital environment, enrich the research experience and make it possible to identify new material easily and to associate it with both a user-defined context and the general index metadata.

But what about the "born digital" data and object? How do we capture it, preserve it, and make it accessible? As we pointed out earlier, digital data is both fragile and ever-changing. For example, according to the Library of Congress, 40 percent of sites available on the Internet in 1998 disappeared a year later.[22] The relative permanence of print products is not matched by the digital production of information. But, equally important, the scale of digital information is phenomenal. To implement persistent and reliable digital archives that record and maintain even a small percentage of our digital information will require a new digital infrastructure, one that is better-suited to accommodating massive storage and massive access demands on it. Libraries are monumental in their structure and their architecture, and ultimately, we need new digital monuments that are as robust and as enduring as our current libraries for our digital environment. Libraries are built and designed as gateways to historical knowledge; they are sites of discovery and learning. The new digital archives will have to fulfill the same functions but they will also have to support the new digital objects. Some of the new digital objects are dynamically generated; in other words, they do not exist as such, but instead are assembled according to a query initiated by a user. How can we record and archive such an object? Or decide on its value for inclusion in a digital archive and determine who should be making such a decision? Most current shopping sites are dynamically generated. Some digital objects are time-sensitive and therefore their preservation requires new protocols to capture them in order to ensure their preservation. And major difficulties arise from maintaining, naming, and authenticating these objects. How are we to convert them in order to keep them accessible with the rapid rate of changes in systems and formats? How are we to develop a naming scheme that will be consistent across archives and networks and finally decide how to authenticate such objects? Security concerns are essential for digital archives because of the nature of the digital object: if integrity of objects is not maintained and authenticated, and repositories are hacked, objects can be modified and tampered with. In this scenario, and we have seen enough security breaches and data modification and loss to realize the importance of secure repositories that will become the template for the accessible digital archives, the legitimacy of the archive itself will become suspect. And if digital archives become not only the record of our digital culture but also the repository of a significant component of our historical and cultural identities, it is crucial to develop and implement their protections.

The digital environment heralds a future of universal access but it also brings increased risks and radical modifications to some essential building-blocks of our cultural activities. It is in the process of converting (both in the technical sense and in the religious sense of the term) our cultural spaces into its own abstractions and categories, and along the way our patrimony and our embedded identities are in the process of becoming more digital. Gateways, interfaces, and access privileges are being transformed from a print-culture-organized world into a world governed by digital literacy and its evolving environment. While digital archives are in the process of being planned for the preservation of cultural heritage, we have also the development and implementation of other archives that have the potential to shape the orientation and deployment of future digital archives.

IV. Digital Hippocrasy: Biometric Data, Retention, and Databases

A growing and controversial set of archives is being implemented as a result of security concerns in the United States and in Europe. Thus we have new demands for more data retention from ISPs and communication services providers, as well as data collected from foreign visitors coming to the United States or biometric data collected for the purposes of issuing proposed biometric passports and biometric Identity Cards.[23] All such efforts, regardless of the politics surrounding their need, are essentially archival projects. They are collections of identifying data that will be used to authenticate identities, or they are the assembly of records of online and other communication transactions that can be mined and analyzed for the purpose of identifying suspicious patterns or other threats. It would seem that we are in the process of developing large-scale archives that are not necessarily that dissimilar from the cultural archives we are interested in in this essay, but on the basis of security and identity controls. Nevertheless, the deployment, albeit early and at times tentative, of such controls affords us a look into the difficulties and the obstacles faced by large-scale archives. These archives also point to the intricate links between some copyright protections, as in the case of databases, and the management of private and confidential information. But the main reason for us to briefly look into their recent history lies in what they tell us about the formation and the reliability of such archives and about their usability and ultimately about their security.

The biometric databases, whether collected from aliens or from citizens for the purposes of secure identification, illustrate the cases of the use of archived data, but also the difficulties with acquiring such data. In the case of the United Kingdom's National ID Act, the Home Office commissioned a biometrics Enrollment Study in order to evaluate and measure the success of acquiring data from individuals.[24] Acquiring data from individuals is perhaps harder than acquiring it from objects, but in both cases, a similar set of problems emerges.

The U.K. trials used a specially designed booth in four major cities: "The biometrics booth was a purpose built oval booth containing the biometric enrollment devices. The camera was mounted on the wall of the booth above a desktop surface. On top of the desktop was an electronic signature pad and sunk into the desktop was the fingerprint device. The participant sat on a standard office chair within the booth while being enrolled, or in the case of wheelchair users in their wheelchair in the booth. The operator sat just outside the booth, but still maintained visual contact."[25] While the generation of biometric data was overall successful, the verification was less promising. For example, facial-recognition verification success rate varied between 69 percent and 48.5 percent (for disabled participants).[26] Such low success rates reflect the difficulties recognition algorithms have in matching the stored image or template against the one presented for verification. But they also represent other factors that come into play, from aging to change in appearance that cannot be easily accounted for in the digital archive. Even fingerprint verification was surprisingly low, at 80 percent. If anything, such mismatches demonstrate the differences between objects and their digital representation or images. They remind us that context and environment are important factors in determining meaning as well as identity. And biometric records have aging problems of their own: the initial database of templates used for verification needs to be refreshed in order to protect it against aging induced by increased use and access. And cultural digital archives will face similar problems with the integrity and reliability of their digitized objects, from aging to accuracy and usability.

A second set of archives, as mentioned earlier, consists of databases assembled by providers of communication services but also by companies that collect, store, organize, and sell publicly available data on citizens, their spending habits, their credit history, and various aspects of their transactional histories. In these cases, some of the collected data is used for management purposes (billing, settlement of claims, etc.), but governments and security agencies are requesting access to the information and demanding its long-term retention in order to mine it for suspicious activities. In this instance, profiling and privacy become the foremost concerns. But we also encounter significant policy changes that are driven by technological availability: if a database is already present and accessible, then it will be exploited through new mining and search tools. Mining databases mirrors the polyphonic and aggregate nature of digital identity: the two are the convergence of the technological abstraction and construction of identity in the digital environment. Privacy and security come into direct conflict in these cases. It remains to be seen if a workable compromise will be achieved.[27] While such conflicts are primarily political and social, there are potential technological solutions on the horizon. One such a solution is the Hippocratic Database.[28]

Hippocratic Databases are important because with the transition to the digital, we will soon have not only cultural digital archives, but also health data and other sensitive information in digital format. Thus a privacy-respecting data-mining instrument is potentially possible and holds tremendous promise if it can be successfully adapted and deployed. Hippocratic Databases are meant for deployment in health, finance, and government, that is to say, either industries that handle and manage sensitive information or public-sector institutions (and we can imagine the use of such databases for cultural and heritage archives). They are designed to take into account privacy, security policies, local legislation, and jurisdictional issues arising from the transfer of data or of jurisdiction over access to data. The strength of the model derives from the fact that such databases automate disclosure rules based on strict implementations of policies, applicable legislation, and user preferences. In other words, they will function the way they are supposed to if there is legislation that provides for explicit digital protection of private information, and one that gives individuals some say about how their confidential data is managed, stored, organized, and accessed, and for what purposes. It seems to me that such a model is a viable one not only for health and financial information, but also for valuable cultural objects and their digitization.

Digital archiving is not only about converting the record of the past into digital form, not only about preserving the digital present: it is also about the future: a future of access, of relevance, and of freedom.

V. Archiving, Privacy, and Literacy

While technological innovations such as the management of databases with a view to the protection of private and confidential information, especially in the health and finance sectors, are but an early indication of the increasing awareness of the need for a comprehensive reflection by both governments and their agencies as well as by technology and access providers, it is also the case that the unprecedented collection of information by providers such as Google has raised some alarming concerns, both in the United States and in Europe. Indeed, the growing transition from a desktop model of computer use to a digital literacy grounded in the social-networking model and based on the distributed Web presence brings about new challenges from the point of view of privacy protections and the regulation of the use of collected data. At the same time, and as we noted earlier, owing to security concerns the same governments are also requesting longer and broader data retention, thus increasing privacy risks.[29] From our perspective, in this chapter at least, such a dual track—the growth of available data collection driven by both normal digital activities and by government requirements—can only serve to highlight the importance of digital archives and the role they can play in the culture at large. First, we will perhaps see a critical examination of the privacy policies and practices of large providers and the associated archiving and management of collected data. Second, and perhaps more significantly, we will witness a slow but ultimately important shift in the accepted norms that define digital privacy and its management both by providers and by users. In this sense, the digital divide we discussed in the first chapter will only become more acute and more prominent because it will reveal the gap between continually changing practices that require more data and more storage and assessment of online history and a legal and ultimately reliable and binding privacy policies. Furthermore, digital literacy, in the fullest sense of the term, will take on additional significance, for it becomes the sole effective framework for a continuous negotiation between the freedom of access and navigation and their consequences from a privacy and security point of view. Software makers and access providers argue that the current trend is at once desirable, beneficial, and in some respects inevitable, and that any stringent definition of privacy in the digital realm will only hinder progress and innovation. It remains nonetheless true, from a user's perspective, that there is a glaring need for a careful and balanced understanding of the implications, for identity management, of digital social practices and the expectations they create, on the one hand; and on the other hand, of the ownership and commercial potential of the resulting archives. For one of the unique characteristics of digital literacy is the fact that it generates data that is archived and whose ownership is either undecided or ambiguous, thus occasioning a continuous negotiation about date accessibility and ownership. Digital archives are not only the archives of print-like creations: they are also the stored histories of individuals and their practices, the histories of social digital trends and the data they generate, along with the manipulations they make possible.

It is precisely because of their nature that digital archives will have to rely not only on legal protections (whether they apply to intellectual property or to private and confidential information) but also on technologies

that are suited to the practices of digital literacy and privacy. To take only
one example, but a telling one, the technology that for instance will host
the future medical information will have to mirror to a large degree a form
of the "social web," especially since this virtual environment has become
the paradigm for the access, exchange, and management of a diversity of
personal information that can be organized and deployed according to a
privacy hierarchy. Expectations of ease of access, of sharing codes and protocols, of portability will inform both the interfaces of the future and the
associated privacy practices and risks. But no matter what, one thing is
certain: the digital archive will continue to grow in size and density while
migrating into new formats and frameworks, thus highlighting the crucial role that will be played by digital literacy. Some technologists have
proposed "Computational Thinking" as the model for the future.[30] "Computational Thinking" seeks to bridge the gap between individuals and
computers by emphasizing abstractions and "fundamentals," that is, a skill
that "every human must know to function in a modern society."[31] But such
a model, despite its lucidity and promise, remains within a framework informed and shaped by an engineering perspective, by a point of view that
works for a convergence between the machine (or the system) and the users. It is, in my opinion, a part of digital literacy, an important and necessary part, but not the sole component of the literate digital life in the
sense I have tried to espouse it in this chapter.

But Computational Thinking has other advantages because it also shows
the way for intelligent and beneficial uses of literacy and the potential of
digital archives. For an example, we can consider the recent reCaptcha.[32]
reCaptcha is remarkable because of what it manages to bring together: a
practice that has been made popular by the need to fight spam and identity
fraud, the availability of large archives of scanned public domain books
that require reading and correction, an Open Access via the social Web to
such archives, and the possibility of combining the convergence of such
tools and features into the production of new and more reliable archived
digital books:

> A CAPTCHA is a program that can tell whether its user is a human
> or a computer. You've probably seen them—colorful images with
> distorted text at the bottom of Web registration forms. CAPTCHAs

are used by many websites to prevent abuse from "bots," or automated programs usually written to generate spam. No computer program can read distorted text as well as humans can, so bots cannot navigate sites protected by CAPTCHAs.

About 60 million CAPTCHAs are solved by humans around the world every day. In each case, roughly ten seconds of human time are being spent. Individually, that's not a lot of time, but in aggregate these little puzzles consume more than 150,000 hours of work each day. What if we could make positive use of this human effort? reCAPTCHA does exactly that by channeling the effort spent solving CAPTCHAs online into "reading" books.

To archive human knowledge and to make information more accessible to the world, multiple projects are currently digitizing physical books that were written before the computer age. The book pages are being photographically scanned, and then, to make them searchable, transformed into text using "Optical Character Recognition" (OCR). The transformation into text is useful because scanning a book produces images, which are difficult to store on small devices, expensive to download, and cannot be searched. The problem is that OCR is not perfect.[33]

In this instance, digital archives, privacy and security, as well as a form of distributed digital citizenship come together to showcase a promising potential of digital literacy at work. Whether such an effort will succeed remains to be seen, but nevertheless it beckons toward the centrality of digital archives and paves the way for their exploitation in an open fashion that can enrich the accuracy of available material and the knowledge it will generate. Ultimately, digital archives are not exclusively storage: they are instead the sites for the production of knowledge and the playfield of an ever more complex and versatile digital literacy driven by the social dimension of the network culture. The challenge of the future will consist in maintaining access to the enriched archives while also preserving essential privacy within a framework that will be open to social uses such as the ones exemplified by reCaptcha. Furthermore, the social dimension of the Web, as we saw earlier, is fundamentally fragmentary and anthological. The new tools that will harness its powers will have to converge the anthological with the literate practices. Digital literacy is the manifestation of the changing status of the archive and the expression of new narrative and historical structures that are in part formed by "Computational Thinking." The digital archive remains nevertheless an activity; it is an institution formed by the new models of reading and authoring. It is the new material support of digital literacy.[34]

Conclusion:
Pierre Ménard's Heirs

Pierre Ménard is an invisible author: he emerges into the limelight barely, and then only thanks to a friend who is also a reader.[1] Otherwise, he remains hidden, unacknowledged and unrecognized, for he chose to author a work he could not sign with his own name. And yet, his surreptitious and most ambitious work is judged to be radical precisely because of its apparent futility and, more so, because of its historical implausibility, not to say impossibility: writing a new a work that was written in the past without wishing to simply repeat it or its words. Why does such a project emerge and how are we to explain its motivation? It would seem that it is in part inspired by what Leibniz terms an "épuisement linguistique."[2] For the poet of the archive, it is not surprising to find a reference to a work that seeks to "better understand how small is man compared to the infinite substance."[3] Instead of the relation between man and the infinite, Borges substitutes the one between an author and the archive, or authorship and the archive, a relation in terms of which an individual can easily lose his identity.

Leibniz focuses on what we may call the Linguistic Singularity: the ut-
terance and its ultimate fate—it is destined to repetition—and its literary
conversion, thanks to variables ranging from context to authorship. If a
day comes when all that is sayable (*énonçable* or *prononçable*, according to
Leibniz) will have been said, thinking remains. What is thought is the
remainder after the exhaustion of linguistic utterances. Ménard's project
is thus significant precisely because of its futility, or because of its apparent loss of identity.[4] According to the narrator, Ménard's fragmentary
Quichotte is the most literate and learned exercise because it points to the
crucial role of reading in the formation of authorship and also because it
demonstrates the transformation brought about by context. Ultimately, it
designates the fragility and the historicity of authorship across cultural
history and across cultures. Ménard is a crypto-author: he does not merely
repeat, word for word, the venerable text of Cervantes, but instead he tells
it from a different perspective; he converts it into a contemporary text. It
is this process of conversion that explains why an essay on digital culture
and its emerging literacy concludes with a discussion of a Borges tale.

In the transitional period in which we find ourselves, Pierre Ménard
would be a prime candidate for piracy and for copyright-infringement
inducement under most Western copyright laws. His literary achievement
is, from a strictly legal point of view, an illegal copy. Because it insists on
an exact and literal reproduction of its original, it is condemned to an illegal status. Thus, Ménard cannot become an author of the *Quichotte* because the *Quichotte* already has an author. But beyond the theoretical piracy of a public domain work, Ménard represents an extreme predigital
case where authorship and identity converge in legal terms and one in
which authorship and reading actually shape the text and its reception. In
other words, Ménard exposes the nature of the print object in its full cultural density. But he also prefigures the manner in which digital technology extends, through the nature of the digital object and its almost infinite conversions, the creative role played by reading as a form of authoring.
He also points the way to a reassessment of the intimate links, inscribed
in the law, between identity, individuality, originality, and ownership of
intellectual property.[5] What is necessary is revealed to be contingent; what
is transhistorical is shown to be the product of a period, of a choice, and
ultimately, subject to change if not disappearance. Ménard's conversion is,

in a sense, an icon and a symptom of what digital literacy and its practices entail.

Thus, the tale invites us to reflect on identity and rights in the hybrid world of digital literacy, its conventions and conversions, its fundamental modification of the relations between the word (or at least its digital manifestation) and its assumed affiliation with a name, an individual, or ultimately a form of property. The seemingly futile literary exercise, destined to disappear under the weight of tradition and its assumptions, exposes significant fissures in the extended model of authorship, its institutions, and its legal incarnations. Conversion, circulating in the unstable confines of Borges's narrative frame, mirrors also the potential embedded within the ever-expanding horizon of digital conversion. The digital palimpsests it calls on are infrastructure-driven by continuous forms of change and displacement, while maintaining a relative stability of access and usability. But along the way, some things have to change. It is in this respect that digital culture is, in my opinion, a reading culture. First, because it provides an environment in which the image and the word share a different if not an altogether new space. They cohabit an emerging site for the production of meaning and knowledge. But they also activate reading, not only as a surreptitious or invisible companion to authorship, but as an equal activity. Such displacements highlight some of the radical and, to some, disturbing implications of the models of circulation and manipulation of the digital objects, and the ways in which they challenge institutionally entrenched forms of authorship.

In his *De l'horizon de la doctrine humaine*, Leibniz observes the possible consequences of the mathematically predictable exhaustion of what is sayable, while carefully distinguishing this finality from what is thinkable. In a similar fashion, digital culture takes off from the limitation of the concepts and categories derived from print and its culture, and those that manage to a significant degree our intellectual economy, heralding not the demise nor the disappearance of the individual and his voice, but new forms governing their relations and their digital appearance and transmission.

It so happens that, even beyond the economic weight of print, authorship has been a core value of an ethics of intellectual property, shaping historical narratives and cherished assumptions concerning individuality, freedom, innovation, and ultimately a "human" dimension that associates our world with our ideas and their various forms of expression. Digital literacy, as I have suggested, radically questions and displaces this model. It first stands for the model's exhaustion and for the rise of the voices of those who are, like Leibniz's, humans, aware that when they repeat what has already been said they are nevertheless thinking and doing differently. Digital literacy, in this sense, is the heir to Pierre Ménard, the secret and invisible author of the *Don Quixote*. The words are the same, but the environment is other. The sentences are similar, but the context is different.

It remains true, however, that digital literacy is still in its infancy: it is seeking its own cultural and legal if not political frameworks. It is an activity with tremendous promise and serious potential limitations, but it is no longer the culture of the future. It is our present.

Borges's fiction is that of a friend with *access* to the *private archive* that alone, it would seem, holds the key to Ménard's secret achievement and unrecognized, masterful authorship. The confrontation of the public and the private reveals the fragile nature of the archive itself: it shows the numerous zones of ambiguity, the multiple areas of ambivalence and confusion as to the true nature of the object, its provenance, its history, its authorship and ownership. If anything, such a learned and literate confrontation exposes the fluidity and the mutability of identity even within the relative fixity of print.

Our confrontation with the digital, although in its early phases, has already opened up the way toward a careful and enlightened evaluation of challenges to established conceptual "comfort zones" ranging from property to authorship and identity. While the digital is by no means a utopia, it is nevertheless our new reality, with its own freedoms and blind spots. It is also without a doubt the future we will make. The question that remains, to recall the epigraph from René Char, with which we began this book, is what kind of testament, if any, precedes it.

Glossary

Notes

Index

Glossary

AJAX: Asynchronous JavaScript + XML. Web developments techniques relying on Open Source tools and frameworks to create interactive online applications, prevalent in Web 2.0 portals and sites.

Anonymity: Can only be relative within the digital environment and refers to the possibility of dissociating data from personal identity, that is, data without an associated identity.

API: Application Programming Interface

Artificial Intelligence: Science of "Intelligent Machines," or the diverse efforts to produce computational equivalents of human intelligence.

Authentication: Verification of stated identity.

Blog: A publishing outlet, organized in reverse chronological order and frequently authored by a single individual.

Biometrics: Automated methods for recognizing an individual based on physiological or behavioristic characteristics. These include: face, fingerprints, hand geometry, iris, retinal, voice, and vein. Handwriting can also be used as a biometric identifier.

Conversion: Changing digital data from one format to another.

Copyright: Intellectual property conventions and laws that regulate the publication, transmission, and modification of original works.

Creative Commons: A set of licenses based on copyright and tailored for the intellectual property management of digital works, based on key concepts such as sharing, commercial use, and reproduction.

CSS: Cascading Style Sheet. Standard mechanisms for adding style elements to Web pages, managed by W3C.

CSS: Content Scrambling Scheme. Encryption scheme developed for the Motion Picture Association of America in order to lock and protect media on DVDs.

Cybertography: Use of digital maps (Google Maps, Yahoo! Maps, etc.) in Web 2.0 applications and portals.

Digital Identity: Digital representation of individual user in a networked environment.

Digital Life Aggregator: Online tools for creating a unified hub or page accessing all digital information (e-mail, news, calendar, RSS feeds, images, videos, etc.).

Digital Rights Management: DRM identifies (ISBN and similar standards that identify books, serials, music, recordings, film, etc.) intellectual property and provides a framework (a set of rules describing acceptable use) for the enforcement of usage restrictions or the exploitation of protected material.

Domain Name System: Management of Internet Registered Domains and the association between IP numbers and human readable addresses.

Encoding: Methods and Formats for the presentation or transmission of digital data.

Encryption: Conversion of digital data into unreadable form. Encrypted data requires a key in order to be reconverted into a readable format.

EULA: End User License Agreement. Contract between software maker or distributor and users that specifies the terms of use of software.

Filtering: Techniques for controlling access to content. Can be used to reduce spam or to censor access to online material.

GPL: General Public License, most widely used Open Source license.

Governance: State and non state decision-making agreements that manage a broad segment of the Internet (DNS, etc.).

Identification: Declaration of identity that may require authentication (or verification).

Identity Management: Tools and methods for creating and maintaining digital presence and associated rights and restrictions.

Indexing: Generation of data meant to facilitate access and retrieval of online objects.

ISP: Internet Service Provider.

Mashup: Site or application combining data from a number of online sources in order to present the user with an enhanced experience (i.e., association of images with geographical data and maps).

Open Access: Publication of peer-reviewed, scholarly material in open digital form.

Peer-to-Peer: Protocol for networking computers in an ad hoc manner in order to maximize sharing and distribution of digital files.

Permalink: Permanent online address of a blog or similar entry.

Phishing: A method for obtaining private and sensitive user data (personal and financial information) for criminal use.

Podcasting: Creation and distribution of digital media files (mostly sound recording) via RSS feeds.

Protocol: Standards for managing connections and data exchange between machines and network nodes.

PKI: Public Key Infrastructure. Infrastructure for the generation, management storage, and retrieval of encryption keys.

Privacy: Culturally determined category. In the digital environment, it refers to users' rights to manage their confidential information and to curtail its distribution and reuse by third parties.

RSS: Format(s) for syndicating online content.

Search engine: Information retrieval system based on hierarchy relevance and the continued indexing of online material.

Security: Protection of digital data and assurance of its integrity through access controls, encryption, or similar methods.

Social Web: Distributed online environment linking individual users or organizations based on mutual agreements and membership.

Spam: Unsolicited e-mails or any other similar digital communication designed to entice users to visit sites or to purchase items online.

SSO: Single Sign-On. A method for identifying and authenticating users for the purpose of managing their access privileges in an online environment.

Tags: Keywords associated with a digital object. Tags may be user or machine generated.

URL: Uniform Resource Locator. Means of identifying and locating digital objects online.

Wi-Fi: Wireless Fidelity. Mostly used to define protocols for accessing mobile computer devices.

Wiki: Collaborative authoring tool allowing for multiple users to access and modify content.

XML: Extensible Markup Language. Markup language for digital content consisting of structured information.

Notes

Note to the American Edition

1. For a more detailed exposition of the anthological, see my "Digital Object-hood and Scholarly Publishing" (ecommons.cornell.edu/bitstream/1813/12020/ . . . / HumPubForum_Doueihi.pdf), and Philip E. Lewis's response to the paper. http:// ecommons.cornell.edu/bitstream/1813/12023/2/HumPubForum_Lewis.pdf. See also "Vers une culture anthologique," *Documentaliste*, 47, no. 1 (2010), pp. 59–60.

2. This also ties in with the ontological or semantic dimension of the Web and the increasingly important role of various learned, scientific vocabularies and folksonomies in shaping our interaction with cultural objects.

3. For a full exposition of this analysis, my forthcoming *Pour un humanisme numérique* (Paris: Seuil, 2011).

4. See Marcel Mauss's pioneering essay published in 1934, *Les techniques du corps*, available from http://classiques.uqac.ca/classiques/mauss_marcel/socio_et_ anthropo/6_Techniques_corps/Techniques_corps.html.

Preface

1. Among the more interesting lawyers, see the work of Lawrence Lessig (http://www.lessig.org), James Boyle (http://james-boyle.com/), and Karl-Friedrich Lenz (http://k.lenz.name/LB/). For scientists and technologists, see Edward Felten's writings (http://www.freedom-to-tinker.com), and Dave Winer's blog

(http://scripting.com). Some interesting efforts, applying "critical theory" to the digital environment, have come to surface in this area. For an example, see the February 2007 issue of *Human Technology: An Interdisciplinary Journal on Humans in ICT Environments* (http://www.humantechnology.jyu.fi), and *First Monday* (http://www.firstmonday.org/). See also Susan Hockey, *Electronic Texts in the Humanities* (Oxford: Oxford University Press, 2000), and Jerome J. McGann, *Radiant Textuality* (London and New York: Palgrave, 2001). For "Digital Humanities," see, among others, Susan Schreibman, Ray Siemens, and John Unsworth, eds., *Companion to Digital Humanities* (Oxford: Blackwell, 2004), and Kathryn Sutherland, ed., *Electronic Text: Investigations in Method and Theory* (Oxford: Oxford University Press, 1997).

2. This obviously has changed since these lines were first written, with the emergence of Digital Humanities.

3. For a recent survey of the standards of literacy that covers also some aspects of digital literacy, see T. Dobson and J. Willinsky's chapter, "Digital Literacy," in *The Cambridge Handbook on Literacy* (Cambridge: Cambridge University Press, 2007). The essay is also available from http://pkp.sfu.ca/files/Digital%20Literacy.pdf.

4. "Le lieu d'où l'on traite de la culture," in *La culture au pluriel* (Paris: Christian Bourgois, 1980 [1974]), p. 219. My translation.

Introduction

1. For Elias, see *The History of Manners* (New York: Pantheon, 1982), *The Civilizing Process* (London: Wiley-Blackwell, 2000), and *The Court Society* (New York: Pantheon, 1982).

2. We will see in Chapter 3 whether it is closer to a monotheism or a polytheism.

3. It has become commonplace to lament the spread of American English that accompanies the success of digital culture. One notable exception is Alain Fleischer, who writes, in his *L'accent: Une langue fantôme* (Paris: Seuil, 2005): "L'incomparable succès de l'anglais ne peut pas s'expliquer par la seule puissance politique, économique et militaire d'un pays dominant comme les États-unis, dont l'influence tient aussi à son rôle de grand inventeur et de grand diffuseur d'innovations technologiques, de produits de toutes sortes, de modèles culturels et comportementaux dans les domaines alimentaire, vestimentaire, cinématographique, littéraire, musical. il faut aussi se rappeler la façon dont cette langue est utilisable, consommable, quelle goût elle a quand on se met dans la bouche, quel son elle produit quand on l'a dans l'oreille" (pp. 66–67). I would simply add that the success of English, at least in the digital environment, is also tied to the technological side and the role English plays in the formation of tools (compilers, etc.) as well as programming languages and standards such as HTML and XML.

4. I will be referring to the definitive edition of Ellul's *The Technological Society* (New York: Vintage, 1964), trans. J. Wilkinson, p. xxxv. It is important to distinguish Ellul's work and thought from those of the Luddites. On the Luddites, see Steve E. Jones's recent *Against Technology* (London: Routledge, 2006).

5. For details of Ellul's analysis, see *The Technological Society*, pp. 85–94.

6. Ibid., p. 128.

7. This dimension, which we will discuss at some length in Chapter 4, devoted to digital archiving, results from the epistemology of error at the core of digital culture: new innovations bring along new problems that require increasingly complex solutions with their own difficulties.

8. For a linguistic discussion of polyphony, see Oswald Ducrot's "Esquisse d'une théorie polyphonique de l'énonciation," in *Le dire et le dit* (Paris: Minuit, 1984), pp. 171–233, especially pp. 172, 197, and 205.

9. For a relevant discussion of an anthropology of credibility in a cultural context, see Michel de Certeau's *La culture au pluriel* (Paris: Christian Bourgois, 1980 [1974]), p. 11.

10. For a critique of Technodiscourse and its underlying rational assumptions, see D. Janicaud's *La puissance du rationnel* (Paris: Gallimard, 1985).

11. For a now classic presentation of this state of affairs, see Albert-Laszlo Barabasi's *Linked: The New Science of Networks* (New York: Perseus Books, 2002).

12. "Who is too blind to see that a profound mutation is being advocated here? A new dismembering and a complete reconstitution of the human being so that he can at last become the objective (and also the total object) of techniques. Excluding all but the mathematical element, he is indeed a fit end for the means he has constructed. He is also completely despoiled of everything that traditionally constituted his essence. Man becomes a pure appearance, a kaleidoscope of external shapes, an abstraction armed with all the sovereign signs of Jupiter the Thunderer." Ellul, *The Technological Society* (New York: Vintage, 1964), pp. 431–432.

13. Martin Heidegger, *Introduction à la métaphysique* (Tel: Gallimard, 1967), trans. Gilbert Khan, p. 171. Technology and its discourse is to be distinguished from poetry, for "La langue est la poésie originelle, dans laquelle un peuple dit l'être" (p. 176).

14. Michel Foucault, *Les mots et les choses* (Paris: Gallimard, 1966). For a version of the disappearance of the author, see Paul Otchackovsky-Laurens, "Des auteurs en voie de disparition," *Le Monde*, April 27, 2006.

15. Michel Foucault, *L'ordre du discours* (Paris: Gallimard, 1971). See also *The Foucault Reader* (New York: Vintage, 1984).

16. Luc Steels, "Digital Angels." http://arti.vub.ac.be/steels/sued-deutsche.pdf.

17. Ibid., p. 13.

18. See http://arti.vub.ac.be/steels/ for a more complete representation of Steels's work and research.

19. Ray Kurzweil, *The Age of Intelligent Machines* (New York: Viking, 1999), and *The Singularity Is Near: When Humans Transcend Biology* (New York: Penguin, 2005). For an up-to-date listing of his research and publications, see http://www.kurzweilAI.net.

20. Ray Kurzweil, "The Future of Machine-Human Intelligence," *The Futurist*, March–April 2006, pp. 39–40.

1. Digital Divides and the Emerging Digital Literacy

1. For a sample of representative reports describing and discussing the digital divide, see www.gatesfoundation.org/nr/Downloads/libraries/uslibraries/reports/TowardEqualityofAccess.pdf, and http://www.unctad.org/templates/webflyer.asp?docid=6994&intItemID=2068&lang=1&mode=downloads.

2. For a recent survey of both online and stand-alone RSS readers, see *The Ultimate RSS Toolbox—120+ RSS Resources*, http://mashable.com/2007/06/11/rss-toolbox/.

3. Some programmers are aware of such an alienation. Thus, in the latest version of NetNewsWire, a desktop RSS Aggregator, a new feature, dubbed Feed Cover Art (in order to compare it to the familiar Music Cover Art) is designed to allow the user to view a snapshot of the sites he is subscribed to: "You can show a thumbnail of the current feed in the lower-left corner of the window. Click the little rectangle button to hide and show the thumbnail. It's kind of like cover art for feeds. The idea is so that you notice when a website re-designs, so that you don't feel too far away from the website, so that you have a visual indication of what feed you're reading." http://ranchero.com/netnewswire/changenotes/netnewswire3.0d46.php.

4. For a reflection of emerging forms of digital authorship, see Lev Manovich's *The Language of New Media* (Cambridge, Mass.: MIT Press, 2001), and especially the updated version of chapter 3 of the book *Models of Authorship in New Media*, http://www.manovich.net/DOCS/models_of_authorship.doc.

5. http://blog.seattlepi.nwsource.com/microsoft/archives/115076.asp.

6. http://eyetrack.poynter.org/. At the point of this writing, only a summary of the report was available online.

7. Steve Jobs, "Thoughts on Music," February 6, 2007, http://www.apple.com/hotnews/thoughtsonmusic/. And here is a response to the article from Macrovision (http://www.macrovision.com/company/news/drm/response_letter.shtml): "As an industry, we can overcome the DRM challenges. A commitment to transparent, interoperable and reasonable DRM will effectively bridge the gap between consumers and content owners, eliminate confusion and make it possible for new releases and premium content to enter the digital environment and kick off a new era of entertainment." Interesting to note that "convenience" is a key term in the potential success of DRM in the digital environment, at least for Microvision. Apple began selling DRM Free Music from EMI on April 2, 2007. For details, see http://www.apple.com/pr/library/2007/04/02itunes.html.

8. FairPlay is the name of Apple's DRM, deployed via iTunes and used on all purchased music from its store and on its iPods.

9. For a study that looks into both the harmonization of copyright laws and the financial viability of the iTunes Store model, see the iTunes Case Study from Harvard's Berkman Center, http://cyber.law.harvard.edu/media/uploads/81/iTunesWhitePaper0604.pdf. It is interesting to note that publishers have resisted such a model in their tentative ventures in online markets.

10. http://news.bbc.co.uk/2/hi/technology/6362069.stm. "Among all record labels 48% of all executives thought ending DRM would boost download sales—

though this was 58% at the larger labels. Outside the record labels 73% of those questioned thought dropping DRM would be a boost for the whole market." And the conclusion of the report's author is most revealing about the attitude of the music industry: "Despite everything that has been happening the record labels are not about to drop DRM. . . . Even though all they are doing is making themselves look even less compelling by using it."

11. We shall return to the question of the city in Chapter 2.

12. French expression for electronic or "virtual" books.

13. For a recent discussion of the peculiarities of the French situation, see Jérôme Vidal's *Sur l'avenir de l'édition indépendante et la publicité de la pensée critique* (Paris: Éd. Amsterdam, 2006).

14. For full details on LWDRM and its current status, see http://www.idmt.fraunhofer.de/eng/research_topics/lwdrm.htm. For an extensive critique of its model and its weaknesses, see Edward Felten's remarks, http://www.freedom-to-tinker.com/archives/000559.html.

15. We shall return to this question in Chapter 4 in the context of a discussion of digital archives.

16. *Universal City Studios v. Corley* [FN191: 273 F.3d 429, 60 USPQ2d 1953 (2nd Cir. 2001)].

17. Some programmers would disagree. For a discussion of elegant and literate code, see Donald Knuth's *Literate Programming* (Stanford, Calif.: Center for the Study of Language and Information, 1992). For another illustration of "Beautiful Code," see http://beautifulcode.oreillynet.com/, and Andy Oram and Greg Wilson, eds., *Beautiful Code* (Sebastopol, Calif.: O'Reilly Books, 2007).

18. Donald Knuth, *Literate Programming*. Emphasis added.

19. Web 2.0 definition is somewhat controversial, but here is a working definition from Wikipedia: "The term 'Web 2.0' (2004–present) is commonly associated with web applications that facilitate interactive information sharing, interoperability, user-centered design,and collaboration on the World Wide Web. Examples of Web 2.0 include web-based communities, hosted services, web applications, social-networking sites, video-sharing sites, wikis, blogs, mashups, and folksonomies. A Web 2.0 site allows its users to interact with other users or to change website content, in contrast to non-interactive websites where users are limited to the passive viewing of information that is provided to them," http://en.wikipedia.org/wiki/Web_2.0. We will return to the significance of a possible transition from Desktop to a more robust and equivalent Web environment. It is also related to the current popularity of AJAX ("a shorthand for Asynchronous Javascript+XML"). For AJAX, see http://adaptivepath.com/publications/essays/archives/000385.php. AJAX is also anthological in that it consists of "several technologies, each flourishing in its own right, coming together in powerful new ways."

20. http://www.apple.com/macosx/leopard/dashboard.html.

21. We shall discuss some of these issues in more detail in Chapter 3.

22. At the time of writing this chapter, rumors of the possible demise of Wikipedia abound, due to financial difficulties. It goes without saying that the discussion of Wikis, while taking into account the remarkable success of Wikipedia, concerns Wikis as a model of authorship in the digital age. At the same time it is

difficult to imagine a "disappearance" of Wikipedia in view of the fact that it has become the first place for reference online. Interesting to note, in this context, the German government's recent decision to fund the authoring of "accurate and reliable" entries about "renewable resources" in the German edition of Wikipedia. For details, see http://www.heise.de/english/newsticker/news/91733.

23. http://www.wikiprofessional.info/.

24. For Twitter, see http://twitter.com/ and for some of the technological add-ons, see especially Dave Winer's work and analysis, http://scripting.com/. A similar service is offered by Jaiku (http://www.jaiku.com), recently acquired by Google.

25. CERT is providing some guidelines for secure code: https://www.secure coding.cert.org/confluence/display/seccode/CERT+Secure+Coding+Standards.

26. Just for a sample of the Business in Computer Security, see the following from Microsoft: http://www.microsoft.com/business/executivecircle/content/article.aspx?cid=2010&subcatid=304, and http://www.microsoft.com/business/executivecircle/content/article.aspx?cid=1951&subcatid=304.

27. See http://blog.wired.com/27bstroke6/2007/02/homeland_securi.html, for full details, including a history of the TSA's official response and ultimate resolution of the issue as well as the collection of extensive and possibly illegal information about visitors. The snapshot is reproduced here courtesy of *27B Stroke 6* Blog.

28. "We believe we're creating a new category," Dennis Bonsall, Microsoft's director of product management for OneCare, said in an interview last week. "It is not about security anymore, but it is about holistic PC care," in "Microsoft shakes up the security tray," http://news.zdnet.com/2100–1009_22–6080718.html.

29. Cell biology has already served as a model for a representation and the development of automated or semiautomated network and computer security defenses.

30. If I choose to privilege this figure, it is in part because of its use by an icon of the digital environment, namely, *Google Scholar* (a service that has generated much controversy): *Stand on the Shoulders of Giants.* The scientific use of the image has its early modern version in the writings of Francis Bacon, then Pascal and ultimately, Newton. The Giants celebrated by Google as its motto is but a variation on a theme that deals with the relations between the Ancients and the Moderns (from Bacon to Pascal, to name only two well-known figures) and that centers on perspective as constitutive of knowledge.

31. For a recent survey of aspects of digital identity that tackles some of the questions raised here in some detail, see the following symposium: http://www .firstmonday.org/issues/issue11_12/schneider/index.html.

32. For details of the U.S. decisions and their reception, see the following: http://www.eff.org/legal/Jurisdiction_and_sovereignty/LICRA_v_Yahoo/, http://www.techlawjournal.com/topstories/2004/20040823.asp, http://www.cdt .org/jurisdiction/.

33. "The OpenNet Initiative is a collaborative partnership of four leading academic institutions: the Citizen Lab at the Munk Centre for International Studies, University of Toronto, Berkman Center for Internet & Society at Harvard Law

School, the Advanced Network Research Group at the Cambridge Security Programme, University of Cambridge, and the Oxford Internet Institute, Oxford University," http://www.opennetinitiative.net/.

34. For details of the study, see http://www.opennetinitiative.net/modules.php ?op=modload&name=News&file=article&sid=78.

35. For an illustration of Chinese redirected traffic, see http://cyber.law.harvard .edu/filtering/china/google-replacements/.

36. http://www.opennetinitiative.net/studies/saudi/.

37. http://googleblog.blogspot.com/2006/02/testimony-internet-in-china.html.

38. This certainly applies to countries like the United States and the United Kingdom where there is no tradition of a national ID or any similar form, outside of a passport.

39. http://www.homeoffice.gov.uk/passports-and-immigration/id-cards/, and http://www.ips.gov.uk/. And for criticisms of the proposed scheme, see, among many others, the following: http://www.privacy.org/pi/activities/idcard/.

40. While the United States does not have a proposed digital identity system, the Department of Homeland Security has developed its US-VISIT program in which it collects biometric data on entering aliens. For a GAO evaluation of the current system, see http://www.gao.gov/new.items/d07278.pdf. According to a DHS official cited in an article in *Wired* (http://www.wired.com/news/technol ogy/0,72792–0.html?tw=wn_index_3), "We have biometric data for over 80 million foreign visitors. We've already denied entry to almost 2,000 people based on the biometrics alone."

41. http://identityproject.lse.ac.uk/, for full analysis and criticism of the government's proposal and its serious technical shortcomings.

42. We will revisit the problems raised by biometric enrollment and its implications for digital archiving in Chapter 4.

43. Such is the case of Microsoft's Passport Services, to name but one example.

44. A good example here is the Liberty Alliance, http://www.projectliberty .org, which was initially a response and an alternative to the now defunct Passport scheme.

45. For details on Shibboleth, see http://shibboleth.internet2.edu/. "Shibboleth is standards-based, open source middleware software which provides Web Single SignOn (SSO) across or within organizational boundaries. It allows sites to make informed authorization decisions for individual access of protected online resources in a privacy-preserving manner."

46. To list some of the proposed digital identity management solutions: PingID (http://www.pingidentity.com/), LightWeight Identity (http://lid.netmesh.org/ wiki/Main_Page), and OpenPrivacy's Reputation Frameworks (http://www .openprivacy.org/reputations/).

47. OpenID (http://openid.net/) is the most prominent of such efforts.

48. A URI is a Uniform Resource Identifier that is commonly used to navigate the Web.

49. "OpenID is an open, decentralized, free framework for user-centric digital identity.

"OpenID starts with the concept that anyone can identify themselves on the Internet the same way websites do—with a URI (also called a URL or web address). Since URIs are at the very core of Web architecture, they provide a solid foundation for user-centric identity.

"The first piece of the OpenID framework is authentication—how you prove ownership of a URI. Today, websites require usernames and passwords to login, which means that many people use the same password everywhere. With OpenID Authentication (see specs), your username is your URI, and your password (or other credentials) stays safely stored on your OpenID Provider (which you can run yourself, or use a third-party identity provider)."

50. Support is growing for OpenID from major players such as AOL (http:// journals.aol.com/panzerjohn/abstractioneer/entries/2007/02/15/aol-and-openid -where-we-are/1406) and Microsoft (http://www.infoworld.com/article/07/02/ 06/HNmsopenid_1.html), and Technorati (http://technorati.com/weblog/2006/ 10/144.html).

2. Blogging the City

1. New models that correspond to the new reality are emerging without any obvious economic model for the press in its transition to the digital environment.

2. Cybertography refers to the growing offerings of participatory public mapping services (Google and Yahoo! maps, etc.) and their manipulations within the digital environment. A good example is to be found at Flickr maps, where tagged photos are matched with locations on Yahoo! maps: http://www.flickr.com/map/.

3. "Second Life is a 3-D virtual world entirely built and owned by its residents. Since opening to the public in 2003, it has grown explosively and today is inhabited by a total of 4,055,732 people from around the globe"; http://secondlife .com/whatis/.

4. For full details on the latest state of the Blogosphere (as of October 2006), see http://www.sifry.com/alerts/archives/000443.html.

5. It has become all too common for newspapers to also host blogs for some of their journalists.

6. For one such case created by Sony for its PSP, see http://www.pspfanboy .com/2006/12/13/fake-blog-admits-it-was-too-funky-fresh/.

7. Émile Benveniste, "Deux modèles linguistiques de la cité," in *Problèmes de linguistique générale II* (Paris: Gallimard, 1974), pp. 272–280. My translations.

8. "A folksonomy is a system of classification derived from the practice and method of collaboratively creating and managing tags to annotate and categorize content [this practice is also known as collaborative tagging, social classification, social indexing, and social tagging. Folksonomy is a portmanteau of folk and taxonomy].

"Folksonomies became popular on the Web around 2004 as part of social software applications such as social bookmarking and photograph annotation. Tagging, which is characteristic of Web 2.0 services, allows users to collectively classify and find information. Some websites include tag clouds as a way to visualize tags in a folksonomy.

"Attempts have been made to characterize folksonomy in social tagging system as emergent externalization of knowledge structures contributed by multiple users. Models of collaborative tagging have been developed to characterize how knowledge structures could arise and be useful to other users, even when there is a lack of top-down mediation (which is believed to be an important feature because they do not need laborious explicit representations as in semantic web). In particular, cognitive models of collaborative tagging can highlight how differences in internal knowledge structures of multiple users can lead to different emergent properties in the folksonomy of a social tagging system." http://en.wikipedia.org/wiki/Folksonomy.

9. For an excellent discussion of this issue, see the series of entries by Jon Udell, http://blog.jonudell.net, especially http://blog.jonudell.net/2007/02/20/whos-got-the-tag-database-truth-versus-file-truth-part-3/.

10. http://word.sc calls itself a "social dictionary" that allows users to "upload [their] photo[s] for any word in our dictionary! Tell [their] friends to look up the word genius and see [their] picture! Tag any word in the dictionary to share with the world how [they] feel about it! Rate words and find other users who like or dislike them too!"

11. For a guide to blogs, see Rebecca Blood, *The WebBlog Handbook* (Cambridge, Mass.: Perseus Publishing, 2002).

12. This illustrates what we called Digital Civil Wars earlier: the abuse or perversion of a technological feature that results either in its elimination or neutralization, despite its obvious potential social applicability and benefit. Instead of having a rich ecosystem organized around TrackBacks, we have a diminished if not an essentially dysfunctional one. Social tools can also easily become tools for antisocial behavior, even (if not more so) in the digital environment.

13. MovableType has recently gone Open Source.

14. For a survey of the latest in blogs and related tools, see *Blogging Toolbox: 120+ Resources for Bloggers*. Some links to the major blogging services and tools: http://www.blogger.com, http://www.typepad.com/, http://www.wordpress.com, http://www.vox.com, http://spaces.live.com/, http://www.wordpress.org, http://www.movabletype.org, etc.

15. For Citizen Journalism, see Shayne Bowman and Chris Willis, *We Media: How Audiences Are Shaping the Future of News and Information* (2003), available in PDF format: http://www.hypergene.net/wemedia/download/we_media.pdf. See Andrew Keen's *The Cult of the Amateur* (New York: Doubleday Currency, 2007) for an essay that purports to show how "the democratization of the digital world is assaulting our economy, our culture, and our values."

16. For a critique of Greek autochthony, see Marcel Détienne's *Comment être autochtone: Du pur Athénien au français racine* (Paris: Seuil, 2003) and his more recent *Les dieux d'Orphée* (Paris: Gallimard, 2007). See also Nicole Loraux's *Né de la Terre: Mythe et politique à Athènes* (Paris: Seuil, 1996). See also Maurice Olender's remarks in his "Étymologie et autochtonie," in *La Chasse aux évidences* (Paris: Galaade, 2005), pp. 134–138.

17. Pierre Vidal-Naquet, *Le chasseur noir* (Paris: Maspero, 1981), p. 329, my translation; and Jean-Pierre Vernant, *Les Origines de la pensée grecque* (Paris: Presses

universitaires de France, 1962), reprinted in *Oeuvres: Religions, rationalités, politique* (Paris: Éd. du Seuil, 2007), vol. 1, pp. 153–238. The literature on the *polís* is overwhelming and I have limited myself to the texts that have shaped my reading of the digital environment.

18. For the political significance and importance of Hestia and the "foyer commun," see Louis Gernet's "Sur le symbolism politique: Le foyer commun," in *Droit et institutions en Grèce antique* (Paris: Flammarion, 1982), pp. 279–305. See also Detienne's analysis in his *Les dieux d'Orphée*, pp. 138–158.

19. Examples are many here. It suffices to think of the numerous blogs and Wikis that address political oppression and censorship from countries such as North Korea, China, and Iran. But also, to single out a more positive usage of the technology as well, the aggregation of representative voices from underdeveloped countries or countries that are victims of internal strife or civil wars, see the Global Voices Online (http://www.globalvoicesonline.org/). "A growing number of bloggers around the world are emerging as 'bridge bloggers': people who are talking about their country or region to a global audience. Global Voices is your guide to the most interesting conversations, information, and ideas appearing around the world on various forms of participatory media such as blogs, podcasts, photo sharing sites, and videoblogs."

20. Some sites that address cyberbullying: http://www.cyberbullying.ca/, http://www.cyberbully.org/. And a sample of laws to address the problem of cyberbullying: http://news.yahoo.com/s/ap/20070221/ap_on_hi_te/cyberbullying.

21. http://en.wikipedia.org/wiki/Cyberbullying.

22. http://news.bbc.co.uk/2/hi/programmes/click_online/6112754.stm.

23. Perhaps the most eloquent critic of the illusion of privacy is David Brin, in his *The Transparent Society: Will Technology Force Us to Choose between Privacy and Freedom?* (Perseus Press, 1998). For Brin, the openness of technology can serve as a protection against potential abuse, but only if all citizens have equal access to all available information. For an opposing view, the EFF's site on privacy: http://www.eff.org/Privacy/.

24. It goes without saying that this phenomenon is not limited to voice recording but extends to all multimedia.

25. This limitation of media players has been recognized and criticized most clearly by Dave Winer, a podcasting pioneer, in an entry on his blog devoted to the ideal podcast player: http://stories.scripting.com/2007/02/21/podcastPlayer .html.

26. Ibid.

27. We will discuss the archive in Chapter 4, and in Chapter 3 we will visit the question of user licenses of their data on collective Web sites or similar services. I have limited myself here to a discussion of Google because it is the most representative of the issues at hand.

28. The classic case is made by Jean-Noël Jeanneney, in his *Quand Google défie l'Europe* (Mille et Une Nuits, 2005).

29. Interesting to note that Google represents itself as the "Organizer and access point of the world's information," http://www.google.com/a/help/intl/en/

admins/customers.html. At the same time, Germany quit the proposed European search engine, Quaero, leaving France as the sole proponent of the project (now defunct).

30. For an economic analysis of this dimension of Wiki culture, see especially Yochai Benkler, *The Wealth of Networks: How Social Production Transforms Markets and Freedom* (New Haven, Conn.: Yale University Press, 2006). Also available online: http://www.benkler.org/wealth_of_networks/index.php/Main_Page, and the recent Don Tapscott and Anthony D. Williams, *Wikinomics: How Mass Collaboration Changes Everything* (New York: Portfolio Hardcover, 2006).

31. For details, see http://citizendium.org/. The name is a combination of citizen and compendium. An interesting precedent, and unfortunately one that is often ignored in the English- speaking world, is *HyperNietzsche*, an Open Source project still in active development and one that combines an advanced technology with credible scholarly publications and access. For details, see http://www.hyper nietzsche.org, or Paolo D'Iorio, *HyperNietzsche* (Paris: PUF, 200). *HyperNietzsche* has since evolved into *NietzscheSource*, http://nietzschesource.org/.

32. While Citizendium seeks to establish an "objective" model of credibility, other Wiki-like projects aim to represent a particular point of view because they perceive Wikipedia itself as prejudiced. One example among many: Conservapedia (http://www.conservapedia.com): "Conservapedia has over 3,800 educational, clean and concise entries on historical, scientific, legal, and economic topics, as well as more than 350 lectures and term lists. . . . Conservapedia is an online resource and meeting place where we favor Christianity and America." In this instance, we witness a convergence of the religious with the national that, curiously enough, culminates in a linguistic prejudice. Thus, the emphasis on American English. In fact, American spelling of English is one of the main "Commandments" of Conservapedia: "As much as is possible, American spelling of words must be used. (You will only be blocked for violating command 5 if you repeatedly change words from American spelling to another spelling.)" http://www.conserva pedia.com/The_Conservapedia_Commandments.

33. http://en.wikipedia.org/wiki/Wikipedia:About#Who_writes_Wikipedia.3F.

34. http://en.wikipedia.org/wiki/Wikipedia:What_Wikipedia_is_not.

35. http://en.wikibooks.org/wiki/William_Shakespeare%27s_Works/Introduc tion.

36. As of April 2007.

37. At this point, the WikiBook appears to have a rather modest purpose: "Perfect for homework use! Alongside some of the plays, there is a plot summary, either act-by-act or scene-by-scene. Be sure to make the most use out of this marvelous collection on facts on Shakespeare's works, along with the works themselves." But it goes without saying that the majority of the readers will probably never read or keep in mind such warnings about the content of the WikiBook. Instead, it is easy to foresee that for most uninformed online readers of Shakespeare, the WikiBook, once completed, will become an online standard edition.

38. Roger Chartier, "Éditer Shakespeare (1623–2004)," *Ecdotica*, no. 1 (2004), pp. 7–23, and Roger Chartier, Peter Stallybrass, J. Franklin Mowery, and Heather

Wolfe, "Hamlet's Tables and the Technologies of Writing in Renaissance England," *Shakespeare Quarterly*, 55, no. 4 (2004), pp. 379–419.

39. Mireille Delmas-Marty, *Pour un droit commun* (Paris: Seuil, 1994), p. 7. My translation.

40. For an articulation of this perspective from a point of view that is both technically and legally directly related to what we are discussing here, see Philippe Aigrain, *Cause commune* (Paris: Fayard, 2005). Also available online from http://www.causecommune.org/.

41. See Delmas-Marty's conclusion entitled "Au pays des nuages ordonnés," pp. 283–284. See also Hubert Damisch, *Théorie du nuage* (Paris: Seuil, 1972).

42. Chapter 5 will be devoted to the digital archives.

3. Software Tolerance in the Land of Dissidence

I borrow the expression "land of dissidence" from Clifford Geertz's *Islam Observed* (Chicago: University of Chicago Press, 1971 [1968]), p. 78.

1. For a discussion of "digital authorship," see the work of Lev Manovitch, especially his *The Language of New Media* (Cambridge, Mass.: MIT Press, 2001) and his essay "Models of Authorship in New Media," available from http://www.manovich.net/DOCS/models_of_authorship.doc.

2. It has become common to refer to Free and Open Source Software as FOSS.

3. Credibility is obviously related to *Credo*.

4. The Greek *Catholicos* means "universal."

5. Bossuet, *Histoire des Variations des Eglises Protestantes* (1688), in *Oeuvres*, vol. 4 (Paris: Didot Frères, 1847); Pierre Bayle, *Dictionnaire historique et critique* (1697) (Geneva: Slatkine, 1969, reprint); Leibniz, *Essai de théodicée sur la bonté de Dieu, la liberté de l'homme et l'origine du mal* (1710) (Paris: Garnier-Flammarion, 1969).

6. DistroWatch (http://www.distrowatch.com) is a site that tracks FOSS operating systems or Linux distributions. SourceForge (http://www.sourceforge.net) is a service that hosts FOSS projects.

7. There exists a Nerd Theology: http://kk.org/writings/nerd_theology.pdf, and also religious versions of Linux distributions. Just for an example, http://www.whatwouldjesusdownload.com/christianubuntu/2007/02/ubuntu-ce-v2x-edgy-screenshots.html.

8. This is generally the thesis in Max Weber's *The Protestant Ethic and the Spirit of Capitalism*, trans. T. Parsons (London: Routledge, 2001 [1904]).

9. Asianux is the name chosen for the operating system, based on Linux, currently under joint development by Asian countries (China, Japan, and South Korea).

10. For a full discussion of this lawsuit and its implications (and a copy of Viacom's official filing against YouTube), see http://www.freedom-to-tinker.com/?p =1136.

11. For a full description of the notion of "free" in Free Software, see http://www.fsf.org/licensing/essays/free-sw.html.

12. Copyleft is a general method for making a program or other work free, and requiring all modified and extended versions of the program to be free as well.

http://www.fsf.org/licensing/essays/copyleft.html. At the time of this writing, the GPL is undergoing modifications in preparation for the release of a new version that takes into account the latest developments in digital technology and practices. For the GPL and its derivatives, see http://www.fsf.org/licensing/ licenses/gpl.html. Addendum: GPLv3 was officially released. For details, see http:// gplv3.fsf.org/, especially within the context of the recent spate of deals between some Open Source companies and Microsoft (http://www.gnu.org/licenses/gpl-faq .html).

13. http://www.fsf.org/licensing/essays/free-sw.html.

14. Eric Raymond's essay, *The Cathedral and the Bazaar*, http://www.catb.org/ ~esr/writings/cathedral-bazaar/cathedral-bazaar/.

15. Dante Alighieri, *De vulgari eloquentia*, ed. and trans. Steven Botterill (Cambridge: Cambridge University Press, 1996). For Dante, the "vulgar" language is not only noble, it is also natural: "Of these two languages, the 'vulgar' is the noblest."

16. For a history of social networks, see http://www.danah.org/papers/works inprogress/SNSHistory.html.

17. http://www.dabbledb.com/.

18. http://www.dabbledb.com/commons/.

19. For the official DVD CCA description and explanation of CSS, see their FAQ: http://www.dvdcca.org/faq.html. For a history of CSS and its hacking and the legal fight that followed, see http://cyber.law.harvard.edu/openlaw/DVD/dvd -discuss-faq.html. DeCSS raises some major questions about private security schemes and their adoption as a standard as well as concerns about the rights of content distributors to restrict and shape users' experience (from Regional Coding to the control of when a user can access the DVD Menu in order to avoid watching Previews). My focus here is, however, very limited, and it goes to show the blind spot behind the overly legal controls of digital practices best illustrated by FOSS.

20. The story can be found in Porphyry, *De Abstinentia*, 2, no. 28, pp. 4–31, 1. A similar narrative is also found in Pausanias' *Description of Greece*, 1, 24, 4 and 1, 28, 10. For full bibliographic references as well as analysis of the two narratives, see J. L. Durand's *Sacrifice et labour en Grèce ancienne* (Paris: La Découverte—École Française de Rome, 1986).

21. I chose not to discuss the economic arguments for and against FOSS and the management of intellectual property. For a view that is critical of the traditional defense of IP "protectionism," see Michele Boldrin and Justin Levine, *Against Intellectual Monopoly* (http://www.dklevine.com/general/intellectual/ against.htm), and Philippe Aigrain, *Cause commune* (Paris: Fayard, 2005).

22. DistroWatch (http://distrowatch.com/) keeps track of at least 100 distributions.

23. This is most visible with the popularity of blogs and the success of services like Flickr.

24. For a discussion of the shift from Free Software offered with computers (mostly mainframes or WorkStations) to the current environment, see B. Hall, "On Copyright and Patent Protection for Software and Databases: A Tale of Two

Worlds," in Ove Granstrand, ed., *Economics, Law, and Intellectual Property* (Amsterdam: Kluwer Publishing Co., 2003).

25. For a discussion of this aspect of digital culture, see Neal Stephenson's *In the Beginning Was the Command Line*, available from http://www.cryptonomicon.com/beginning.html.

26. For a history of Free and Open Source licenses, see Chris DiBona, Sam Ockman, and Mark Stone, eds., *Open Sources: Voices from the Open Source Revolution* (Sebastopol, Calif.: O'Reilly Publications, 1999). For the GPL and its history, see http://www.gnu.org/gnu/manifesto.html and http://www.gnu.org/licenses/gpl-faq.html. And for more details about BSD, see Andrew Leonard's "BSD Unix: Power to the People, from the Code," http://archive.salon.com/tech/fsp/2000/05/16/chapter_2_part_one/index.html.

27. For one listing of such licenses, see http://www.fsf.org/licensing/licenses/.

28. For an excellent survey and comparison of the major Free and Open licenses in French, see Isabelle Vodjani's *Comparatif de licenses libres: Le choix du libre dans le supermarché du libre choix*, http://www.transactiv-exe.org/spip.php?article95. See also Cyril Rojinsky and Vincent Grynbaum, *Licenses libres et droit français* (2002), available from http://www.grynbaum.com/IMG/pdf/licenceslibres_pi_juillet-2002.pdf.

29. For Documention, see http://www.fsflicensing.org//licenses/index_html; for FreeDocumentationLicenses, see http://artlibre.org/licence/lal/en/; and for an Open Content license, see http://freecontentdefinition.org/Definition.

30. For the full text of the proposal, see http://www.desirsdavenir.org/commun/pdf/RapportRocard.pdf.

31. *République 2.0*, http://www.desirsdavenir.org/commun/pdf/RapportRocard.pdf , pp. 51–52. My translation.

32. It is important to distinguish between Open Access as a general attitude toward information online and the formal movement known as Open Access, one with a specific agenda.

33. This of course does not imply a restricted view of Creative Commons. I only mean to point out the cultural history of the movement. For details about Creative Commons, see http://creativecommons.org/about/history.

34. "Unlike the GNU GPL, Creative Commons licenses are not designed for software, but rather for other kinds of creative works: websites, scholarship, music, film, photography, literature, courseware, etc." http://wiki.creativecommons.org/FFAQ#Can_CC_give_legal_advice_about_its_licenses_or_help_with_CC_license_enforcement.3F.

35. Article I, Section 8 of the Constitution states that the Congress shall have power to "promote the progress of science and useful arts, by securing for limited times to authors and inventors the exclusive right to their respective writings and discoveries."

36. See http://creativecommons.org/worldwide, for details about the international Creative Commons. It is interesting to note, in this context, that the different jurisdictions are compared to different operating systems: "Imagine the licenses as the Legal Code processed by the respective legal 'operating systems' of various jurisdictions. . . . It is the aim of International Commons to 'port' or

adapt the licenses for use across those different operating systems. This will involve both the literal and legal translation of the licenses by teams of volunteers in various jurisdictions around the world." In this instance, the digital has become the guiding metaphor for the legal framework it is modifying through the practices it makes possible. Licenses are portable, much like code.

37. http://sciencecommons.org/resources/faq/sciencecommons.html.

38. For a comprehensive guide to Open Access, see Peter Suber's blog, *Open Access News*, http://www.earlham.edu/~peters/fos/fosblog.html. For a definition and discussion of Open Access, see also his *Open Access Overview* (http://www.earlham.edu/~peters/fos/overview.htm).

39. For the text, see http://www.soros.org/openaccess/read.shtml. The initiative has received two further adaptations known as the Bethesda (http://www.earlham.edu/~peters/fos/bethesda.htm) and Berlin (http://oa.mpg.de/openaccess-berlin/berlindeclaration.html) statements.

40. http://www.soros.org/openaccess/read.shtml.

41. One early pioneer in this field is ArXiv, http://arxiv.org/.

42. Such a desire does not amount to the abandonment of "peer review" of published material. It simply recognizes the fact that scientists tend to present ready-to-publish texts that require little if any journal-supplied editorial assistance.

43. From the Berlin Statement: "Our organizations are interested in the further promotion of the new open access paradigm to gain the most benefit for science and society. Therefore, we intend to make progress by encouraging the holders of cultural heritage to support open access by providing their resources on the Internet . . . [and] advocating that open access publication be recognized in promotion and tenure evaluation." http://oa.mpg.de/openaccess-berlin/berlin declaration.html.

44. The report is available from http://www.acls.org/cyberinfrastructure/OurCulturalCommonwealth.pdf.

45. Most of the digitization projects singled out by the project provide somewhat outdated and ultimately restrictive access to their material. For an example of controlled access to scholarly journals, see Project Muse from the Johns Hopkins University Press (http://muse.jhu.edu). The project, obviously, is not Open Access.

46. For full details, see http://ocw.mit.edu. The project is made available under a Creative Commons Noncommercial-ShareAlike license.

47. http://ocw.mit.edu/OcwWeb/Global/AboutOCW/about-ocw.htm.

48. Most prominent here is Duke University's Digital Initiative (http://www.duke.edu/ddi/itunes/duke.html).

49. http://www.duke.edu/ddi/itunes/duke.html.

50. For details of Google's announcement, see http://googleblog.blogspot.com/2007/08/joining-oin.html, and for the OIN, see http://www.openinventionnetwork.com/.

51. Pascal, *Pensées*, fragment 19, in *Oeuvres complètes* (Paris: Gallimard, Pléiade, 2000), p. 547 ("Ainsi les tableaux vus de trop loin et de trop près. El il n'y a qu'un point indivisible qui soit le véritable lieu, les autres sont trop près, trop loin, trop

haut ou trop bas. La perspective l'assigne dans l'art de la peinture. Mais dans la vérité et dans la morale qui l'assignera?").

4. Archiving the Future

1. http://www.msnbc.msn.com/id/17702021/.

2. http://www.variety.com/article/VR1117963533.html.

3. For the Long Tail, see Chris Anderson's *The Long Tail: Why the Future of Business Is Selling Less of More* (New York: Hyperion, 2006). An early article appeared in *Wired* (October 2004) and is available: http://www.wired.com/wired/archive/12.10/tail.html. Also, see some of Clay Shirky's writing, as, for an example, *Power Laws, Weblogs, and Inequality*, http://www.shirky.com/writings/powerlaw_weblog.html.

4. http://www.archive.org/web/web.php, and for details about the archive and its history, see http://www.archive.org/about/faqs.php#The_Wayback_Machine. Some sites generated by databases are not indexed and archived. The Index takes note only of static pages and cannot record dynamically generated content.

5. For details about Robots.txt, see http://www.robotstxt.org/wc/faq.html.

6. Internet Archive, the owner of the Wayback Machine, now proposes a for-pay archival service designed for cultural institutions: "As information is increasingly digitally created, communicated, and consumed, memory institutions such as archives, libraries and museums face a daunting task of preserving endless quantities of web material. Internet Archive has already recognized this challenge and today released Archive-It 2.0, the latest version of their subscription-based archiving service. Serving a broad range of scholarly organizations at a cost significantly lower than other archive platforms, Archive-It 2.0 enables subscribers to collect, manage, search and preserve online material from their own institutions' websites as well as from the world wide web." http://www.archive.org/iathreads/post-view.php?id=59978.

7. "Today, we're pleased to announce the launch of Web History, a new feature for Google Account users that makes it easy to view and search across the pages you've visited. If you remember seeing something online, you'll be able to find it faster and from any computer with Web History. Web History lets you look back in time, revisit the sites you've browsed, and search over the full text of pages you've seen. It's your slice of the web, at your fingertips. How does Web History work? All you need is a Google Account and the Google Toolbar with PageRank enabled. The Toolbar, as part of your browser, helps us associate the pages you visit with your Google Account. If you're currently a Search History user, you'll notice that we've renamed Search History to Web History to reflect this new functionality." http://googleblog.blogspot.com/2007/04/your-slice-of-web.html.

8. http://www.secondlife.com/.

9. http://books.google.com/intl/en/googlebooks/about.html. Part of the negative reactions to the project stem from its Open-out model based, at least according to Google and its supporters, on fair use.

10. "Google Books Library Project—an enhanced card catalog of the world's books." Ibid.

11. For details on Gallica, see http://www.bnf.fr/pages/zNavigat/frame/infopro.htm?ancre=numerisation/po_chartegallica.htm, and for Europeana, see http://www.europeana.eu/.

12. http://www.microsoft.com/presspass/exec/trubin/03–05–07AmericanPublishers.mspx.

13. Rubin fails to mention that Turning the Page will run only (at least so far) on Internet Explorer and Windows machines: "Turning the Pages 2.0™ allows you to 'virtually' turn the pages of our most precious books. You can magnify details, read or listen to expert commentary on each page, and store or share your own notes. Turning the Pages 2.0™ runs with Internet Explorer on Windows Vista or Windows XP SP2 with. NET Framework version 3, on a broadband connection." http://www.bl.uk/ttp2/ttp2.html.

14. Ibid.

15. *République 2.0*, p. 21.

16. For the article, see http://business.timesonline.co.uk/tol/business/article1294870.ece. And for an insightful commentary on Google's future plans, see Nate Anderson's "Google Book Search: Buy Your Books by the Chapter," http://arstechnica.com/news.ars/post/20070123–8685.html.

17. There is also a French report, *La diffusion numérique du patrimoine, dimension de la politique culturelle*, available from http://www.culture.gouv.fr/culture/actualites/rapports/ory-lavollee/ory-lavollee.pdf. The United Kingdom's NDAD provides access to government data sets and documents, http://www.ndad.nationalarchives.gov.uk/. Taiwan's digital archives can be accessed at Amest://www.ndap.org.tw/index_en.php. These are just two examples among many.

18. http://www.digitalpreservation.gov/ for information about the project and its plans.

19. As, for instance, in the case of Pierre Bayle's *Dictionnaire historique et critique*, http://artfl-project.uchicago.edu/content/dictionnaire-de-bayle.

20. "One issue that can not be adequately addressed here is an ongoing topic of discussion at the Library: the potential for digital versions to serve as preservation copies. Traditionally, preservation of content has focused on creating a facsimile, as faithful a copy of the original as feasible, on a long-lasting medium. The most widely accepted method for preserving the information in textual materials is microfilming and for pictorial materials is photographic reproduction. One aspect of the discussion relates to the question of when it is appropriate to generate a digital version that attempts to be a faithful copy of an item and when to take advantage of the potential for enhancing access to the content. Should the legibility of a manuscript page be improved by adjusting the contrast? For a photographic print, the faithful copy may be most appropriate. However, if the Library owns the negative but no print, is it appropriate to make digital adjustments to sharpen the image for presentation? Can general principles be developed to guide such decisions?" *Historical Collections for the National Digital Library*, http://www.dlib.org/dlib/april96/loc/04c-arms.html.

21. DOI, or the Digital Object Identifier: "The DOI System is for identifying content objects in the digital environment. DOI® names are assigned to any entity for use on digital networks. They are used to provide current information, including where they (or information about them) can be found on the Internet. Information about a digital object may change over time, including where to find it, but its DOI name will not change. The DOI System provides a framework for persistent identification, managing intellectual content, managing metadata, linking customers with content suppliers, facilitating electronic commerce, and enabling automated management of media. DOI names can be used for any form of management of any data, whether commercial or non-commercial." http://www.doi.org/.

22. http://www.digitalpreservation.gov/importance/.

23. For the EU's Data Retention Directive, see http://eur-lex.europa.eu/LexUriServ/LexUriServ.do?uri=CELEX:32006L0024:EN:NOT. The United States does not currently have such a law, but a new one is proposed. The U.S. VISA Program, run by the Department of Homeland Security, collects biometric data from visitors to the country, http://www.dhs.gov/xtrvlsec/programs/content_multi_image_0006.shtm. The United Kingdom has proposed a Biometric Passport as well as a national ID, http://www.opsi.gov.uk/ACTS/acts2006/20060015.htm.

24. http://www.passport.gov.uk/downloads/UKPSBiometrics_Enrolment_Trial_Report.pdf.

25. Ibid., p. 8.

26. Ibid., p. 10.

27. For details about privacy concerns and criticisms of data retention, see http://www.epic.org/privacy/intl/data_retention.html.

28. For details on this research, see http://www.zurich.ibm.com/pri/projects/hippocratic.html.

29. For but one example, see the recent investigation of Google launched by the EU and the issue of data retention (http://www.eweek.com/article2/0,1895,2145907,00.asp), and Google's initial official response (http://64.233.179.110/blog_resources/Google_response_Working_Party_06_2007.pdf).

30. For details on Computational Thinking, see http://www.cs.cmu.edu/computational_thinking.html. The concept was devised by Jeannette Wing.

31. http://www.cs.cmu.edu/afs/cs/usr/wing/www/publications/Wing06.pdf.

32. http://recaptcha.net/.

33. http://recaptcha.net/learnmore.html.

34. Another similar manifestation of the convergence of digital literacy and security and privacy is "disemvoweling," a literate practice that relies on readability: "Reducing readability in order to combat trolling: the increasing reliance on expanded forms of literacy, their automated reception and, ultimately, their visual appearance, as a sign of digital status and legibility. While the text, thus treated, appears gibberish to automated trolls, it is perfectly legible for humans, albeit with some effort and concentration. In this case, digital literacy puts into play both the language and its users as well as discursive digital representation. A liter-

ate user is one who has eyes not only to read, but also to read 'disemvoweled' text, that is to say one who can fill in the blanks, based on a cursory parsing of the visible text. Such an exercise is not far from the literary practices of the Surrealists and of Oulipo, especially Georges Perec. The missing vowel(s) become thus the occasion of interpretation and the site for interactive exchange." http://en.wiki pedia.org/wiki/Disemvoweling.

Conclusion

1. All references to Borges's text are to *Collected Fictions*, trans. Andrew Hurley (Putnam, 1998), pp. 88–95.

2. "A linguistic exhaustion"; Leibniz, *De l'horizon de la doctrine humaine*, translated and annotated by M. Fichant (Paris: Vrin, 1991), pp. 38–39. Leibniz figures prominently in the list of Ménard's works ("Une monographie sur la *Characteristica Universalis* de Leibniz [Nîmes, 1904]," *Fictions*, p. 42).

3. Leibniz, *De l'Horizon*, p. 38 ("mieux concevoir combien peu est l'homme au prix de la substance infinie").

4. "There is no intellectual exercise that is not ultimately pointless. A philosophical doctrine is, at first, a plausible description of the universe; the years go by, and it is a mere chapter—if not a paragraph or proper noun—in the history of philosophy. In literature, that 'falling by the wayside,' that loss of 'relevance' is even better known." Borges, *Collected Fictions*, p. 94.

5. Conversion also plays a role in Borges's narrative.

Index